OPERATORS ARE STANDING BY!

Use the Power of Infomercials and TV Marketing to Sell Your Products and Keep Customers Calling

Michael Planit

D1564897

McGraw-Hill
New York   Chicago   San Francisco   Lisbon
London   Madrid   Mexico City   Milan   New Delhi
San Juan   Seoul   Singapore   Sydney   Toronto

1 2 3 4 5 6 7 8 9 0   FGR/FGR   0 9 8 7

ISBN-13: 978-0-07-147028-5
ISBN-10: 0-07-147028-X

The cover design was created by Adcom Advertising

Permission to use the logo "As Seen on TV" is given by Adcom Advertising.

This publication is designed to provide accurate and authoritative information in regard to the subject matter covered. It is sold with the understanding that the publisher is not engaged in rendering legal, accounting, or other professional service. If legal advice or other expert assistance is required, the services of a competent professional person should be sought.
–From a declaration of principles jointly adopted by a committee of the American Bar Association and a committee of publishers.

McGraw-Hill books are available at special quantity discounts to use as premiums and sales promotions, or for use in corporate training programs. For more information, please write to the Director of Special Sales, Professional Publishing, McGraw-Hill, Two Penn Plaza, New York, NY 10121-2298. Or contact your local bookstore.

Jan, you have inspired me at so many levels, showing me we can do it all: live, love, and laugh, all the while working and raising a family. You are my true inspiration, and it "all" could be done only with you there to help. You are the best wife and mother, and I thank you for your never-ending belief and support in me during this book development process—not to mention during every other product, business concept, plan, and idea that I have ever conjured.

"This is the one!"

Of course, to my kids: Blayne, for showing me to never be afraid to express my ideas and think differently from the crowd—you are a true original, and the most ingenious young lady I know. Jordan, for showing me that it never makes sense to give up because eventually "they" will cave in and you will get what you set out for. Spencer, for showing me that you can be smart, tough, and still be all heart.

You three are my best creations: The returns are incredible, and I love you all.

Contents

Preface

Having grown up in a world of concepts and hot products, I have become attuned to them. I learned early on that the world was full of good ideas, and everybody had one—his or her own dream, his or her own idea. I call it the MOST: My One *Simple* Thing. Just about everybody has his or her own MOST, and usually it is not that *simple.* My father had a million of these ideas. He was always chasing the dream, always looking for the product that would be the MOST for him.

But my dad was not an innovator; he was an "opportunator"— one who takes advantage of, or capitalizes on, trend-oriented opportunities to make money. He saw it, "got it," and acted on it. He had a knack for understanding trends in the marketplace, and he knew that they would be short-lived. He seized the moment, didn't stop to think about it, or better yet, didn't stop to think about the obstacles he would encounter, and just pushed forward and got going—without hesitation.

> When you conceive your idea, it's not so much that you have to act fast, as it is simply that you have to *act*—period.

My father had an ability to recognize a trend and act on it. Of course, he knew there would be obstacles he would encounter along the way—whether unexpected costs, manufacturing delays, or something he couldn't even fathom yet—but he never let them limit the scope of his thinking.

Just like my father, I wanted more from life. (And if you picked up this book, you most likely do too.) I didn't just want to work for a living; I wanted to develop and to create. I wanted to bring new, innovative ideas to reality, from the ground up—I wanted to create *my* own success. I wanted to be an inventor, innovator, and opportunator all in one. I wanted to realize my *own* dream, my own MOST. And now, I want to pass on what I have learned to you so that you can now realize your own dream.

You should not stop to think and worry about the obstacles. There will be some; count on it. But if you let those obstacles get in the way, you will miss out on developing a truly untarnished, fresh concept of your very own.

If you believe in your own MOST enough, just *keep moving, always keep moving*. Never stop working your way around any obstacle, and never stop believing in yourself. And when you hit the wall (and we all hit the wall)—push harder, believe more. Remind yourself why you began, and always keep pushing. Your idea may seem simple—some may view it as silly or unnecessary—but what makes it a great idea in the first place may very well be that it's something no one else is doing.

You'll first want to realize your concept. I understand you're excited; you want it to "come alive." So keep that goal in mind, and do yourself a favor: Do not get hung up on the making-money aspect. In time, the money will come. With hard work and perseverance, you'll definitely see your first success.

> If your product is a trend-oriented product, a hot-for-now item, be prepared to get in and get out. If you cannot move quickly to enter the market, then do not go in at all. Trends are tough—they happen fast, and dissipate even faster.

WHAT CAN THIS BOOK DO FOR YOU?

Starting in the introduction and the first chapter, I will begin to walk you through the product development stage, help you understand the process, and even help you understand your product better than you thought you did. Understand, it is not always the product itself that is important but also who and what purpose it serves and how you position it in the market—not to mention how you get it out there into the marketplace.

As you begin to understand these concepts, you will be challenging yourself, your idea, and all of your preconceived notions of your invention, infomercials, and the retail market. It's possible you will find DR marketing isn't right for your product. Or perhaps you'll discover that this product needs an outlet like HSN or QVC, and we'll talk about how to get you and your invention there!

While the many chapters cover all the details of tackling this project on your own, they also explain real-world truths—for example, you will likely need many partners along the way. But you will be armed and ready to jump into the fray and to enjoy yourself through every step of this exciting journey.

Operators Are Standing By! is separated into two parts. The first part takes you through the creative process. What is your idea? Is your invention right for selling on TV? How do you create a working prototype? What *is* a working prototype? How do you protect your concept? All of this, and more, is covered in Part 1.

Part 2 takes you through what could be the confusing maze of DR TV: everything from direct response marketing techniques to fulfilling and tracking orders, from finding a manufacturer to understanding the differences between the specific needs of long-form and short-form infomercials, and even the dos and don'ts of the pros who have made a living in this wondrous DR TV world.

Before we begin, here's one final word: Your first concept may be the only one you ever need—it may make you more successful than you had ever dreamed possible. But even if you go on to make millions the very first time, you will find yourself hooked. That's right. You will want to do it again (see "The Cycle of Successful Product Development" in Figure P–1). And if you don't make *millions* the first time, that doesn't mean you aren't successful, and it certainly does *not* mean you won't make money. Instead, consider that you

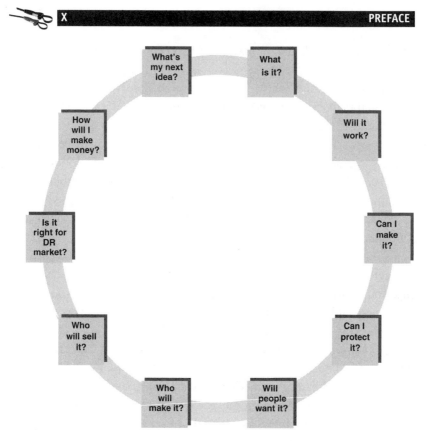

Figure P–1   The Cycle of Successful Product Development

have proven to yourself, and the world, that, when it comes to consumer products, you bring value—you are, at that point, *officially* a proven innovator—an achiever!

Acknowledgments

Robert Potter, without you I would never have begun, and without you I would never have finished. Your contributions, from the preparation of the original treatment to the visual aspects to coincide with my words, is what made this book a reality. Words cannot express my thanks (only because I ran out of them). The journey has been fun, though tiresome at times. I know that, because of your verve and enthusiasm, every endeavor you undertake will achieve the utmost in success.

My brother, Keith Planit, your editing skills and writing direction were a tremendous part of my ability to complete this book. Thank you for staying the course, and thank you for sharing in the process. I look forward to our next book project together.

Russ Lyster, without our shared repartee at dinner well over a year ago, I would not have had the chance to meet my literary agent, Ian Kleinert.

Ian, thank you for your determination and belief in my concept and for finding such a great home for it. I look forward to a long, prosperous relationship with you and your company.

Donya Dickerson, a special thanks for your belief and *patience* in this endeavor. I am honored to have McGraw-Hill as the publisher, and without you, Pattie Amoroso, Tama Harris, and the rest of your team, I could have never achieved what I have. Thank you.

To all those in the industry who have helped guide me and teach me, as well as those who took the time to provide their expert opinions and advice to share with my readers, a special thanks also.

AJ Khubani (founder and president of Telebrands Corporation), thank you for taking (dragging) me into the business and for being open to sharing and teaching. As you are always creating new ways to attract the consumer, sell products, and increase revenues, I have found you to be a true marketing innovator whose particular genius continues to inspire and motivate me.

Andy Khubani (founder and president of Ideavillage LLC), thank you for providing me the opportunity to put into action my particular expertise in strategic marketing and business strategies, while providing me with insights to your methodical and diligent approach toward DR marketing. Without those opportunities, I would never have learned the necessary industry details to experience the successes I have had within the business. I am proud to have shared in and been a part of driving so many successes with you and your company.

Thank you to Tom McLinden (EVO Design); Jason Falk (Tank Industries); Jason Drangel (Epstein Drangel Bazerman & James, LLP); Denise DuBarry Hay (cofounder of Thane International, Inc.); Wendi Cooper (C-Spot Run Entertainment, Inc.); Tara Borakos (Tara Productions, Inc.); Marcia Waldorf (Waldorf-Crawford); Mike Sobo (president of SAS Group); Victor Wai (factory owner, China); Kimberly Fairfield-Frieders (West Corporation); Dick Wechsler (Lockard & Wechsler Direct); and Ron Popeil (founder of Ronco Corporation).

And further thanks to Peter D. Murray, Esq., of Cooper & Dunham LLP, for the additional work in providing the "once-over" on the patent information in Chapter 4. It was greatly appreciated.

A special thanks to the Electronic Retailing Association (ERA) and Barbara Tulipane (president and CEO) and Molly Alton-Mullins (vice president of communications) for their time and for providing all of the insightful and helpful factual information included in Appendix G. And, more importantly, thank you for helping all inventors by providing a truly safe haven for introducing products to the marketplace through infomercial and electronic marketing. Through your efforts, you have helped many inventors follow the path from concept to reality, which has made it possible for them to realize their dreams and their MOST.

Thank you to Don Braca, founder and president of Adcom Advertising, Inc., and Al Cavallo, VP of Creative, for the phenomenal cover design. As originators of the "As Seen on TV" logo and creators of the many retail package designs for many of the successful DR products, I continue to admire and respect your hard work and efforts on behalf of our industry.

Introduction

You are just about to click the remote and change the channel when something on the screen holds your attention. It's late at night, and the bluish light of the television flickers in a darkened room as broadcast programming has come to a close. The hour of the infomercial has arrived.

The spokesperson has promised an unbelievable demonstration you want to stick around and see. The product is exactly what you need to make your life that much easier. You catch yourself staring at the screen, thinking that somebody is probably going to make a million dollars from this product, and all the while you know that the idea that's been percolating in the back of your mind would work even better. It's a product that can make people's lives even easier; a concept that can make a million dollars!

But where do you begin?

You begin with this book. This is the book for every would-be inventor or designer who has ever dared to dream of bringing his or her very own product to the public through the world of *direct response marketing*—infomercials.

There are thousands of individuals out there with strong and novel ideas; there are thousands more sitting on their revolutionary product ideas who don't even know where to begin.

The information and tools I will supply to you in this book have applications far beyond infomercials and direct response marketing and provide valuable insights for anyone, anywhere, trying to sell anything. More so, it offers powerful examples for all those looking to achieve their dreams on their own terms.

And if perchance you don't have an idea just yet, this book will inspire you to tap into your creative potential and then guide you through the steps you need to turn your Big Idea into a reality—the journey that makes your dreams come true.

I started with ideas and dreams, just like anyone else. Learning about the direct response market has allowed me great opportunity to develop products and work on many fun products like the Boogie Bass novelty singing fish (#1 short form, 2000[1]), the Trikke (one of *Time for Kids* magazine's "Best Inventions," 2002), and the Dancing Baby toy line based on the character from the popular 1990s TV series *Ally McBeal.* I also had my hand in bringing to market the Grip-Wrench strap wrench, the Edgemaster paint roller, the Finishing Touch ladies' hair trimmer, the Over Easy Flip Pan, Dermafresh handheld skin-care product, and Smart Tape, the world's first digital read-and-record tape measure (ERA's "Best Short-Form Product," 2003), which I personally designed, developed, and marketed.

These and many other experiences have taught me the fundamentals of the exciting and complex world of being an inventor in today's retail market. In this book I'm going to use the tools I have acquired to provide you with everything you need—from the idea stage to the infomercial soundstage. We will do more than simply outline the convoluted process of a patent application or discuss a bare-bones account of how to develop your invention. We will do more than just list resources for your marketing needs. We will provide a a combination of all these things. But wait . . . there's more!

Filled with necessary information, practical advice, and even sample legal forms and standard formats, this book is also enjoyable reading. It is peppered with real-world accounts from my own experience as well as from other industry professionals, describing in detail our own successes and failures—and the lessons to be learned from them. The book has also been constructed as a "flowchart to marketing success," so you can go straight to the sections that are vital and pertinent to what you are doing, to start reading at exactly the point of the process where you need assistance and motivation.

---

[1] *2000 GreenSheet Spot Report*, Jordan Whitney, Inc.

What this book will bring you is a wealth of knowledge and understanding of direct response marketing. And—with some luck, diligence, and a bit of good old-fashioned ingenuity—it will also bring you much success. So get that thinking cap on because we're about to make *you* a successful inventor.

PART 1

THE PRODUCT

The Cycle of Successful Product Development

1

The Concept Stage

There are a lot of people out there like you and me who have that dream and want to—*must*—make that dream a reality. This is where it all begins: the idea stage.

You saw something, experienced something, or just one day woke up with an idea for something. Either way, you now have "it"—that million-dollar idea. But now what? Can you create it? How do you get it out of your head and into reality? Is it appropriate to be marketed and sold on TV? Will it really work? If you want it, does that mean others will too? And let us not forget: Can you make money from it?

Every aspect of success in direct response marketing (DR marketing) ultimately stems from the idea itself. The first thing we need to do is explore the concept from top to bottom and isolate its strengths and weaknesses. So let's begin by looking at every facet of your idea. The more you can perfect your product now—in the concept stage—the easier everything else will be afterward.

COMING UP WITH YOUR IDEA

Many of you may already have an idea in mind and are anxious to get started on the next steps. Please feel free to skip ahead to "Developing Your Idea" on page 10. This section is for the rest of you—those who simply know they want to create or develop something within a certain area but haven't yet come up with a concept. So let's first discuss how to come up with a successful product idea, one that is right for DR marketing.

Ideas can come from anywhere around you. Maybe it comes to you while you're working. Or maybe you see something at the school your children attend, or at the park, or while watching television, or while sitting in traffic, or while shopping. Maybe you hit upon a way to save money, a way to make an existing product cheaper, an existing *process* more efficient. Perhaps the idea will come out of something people do or use regularly but could be, somehow, done better. Of course, it's possible that the idea will take form as something that doesn't yet exist at all—a truly *new* product!

The point is, good ideas can come from anywhere, at any time— what is important is learning to recognize what makes a good concept and learning to separate the good concepts from the rest.

Many times, the first step in coming up with a good concept is to *identify* an area you are already familiar with and *exploit it*. This doesn't mean you have to be an expert in some kind of scientific or professional area. Do you like to go to football games? Do you like planting flowers? Anything—and I mean *anything*—can lead to ideas.

Next, look within this familiar area and find something that can add to the situation—making it easier, better. For example, years ago, while cooking, someone identified the difficulties that arise in draining the boiling water from a hot pot of pasta, and this person came up with an idea to add a new detail to the pot to make it better. By creating a lid with holes in it that makes it act as a built-in strainer, the inventor created the means to avoid messes, hassles, and possibly scalding burns. The inventor exploited a very familiar and difficult situation. Million-dollar ideas can literally come from anywhere.

The best thing is to *find a problem* or a familiar frustration that could use improvement. Sticking with the cooking theme, for example, consider the procedure of trying to flip omelets like the pros, and failing that, making ordinary scrambled eggs. Someone noted these difficulties and created a product to help the cook overcome them. The observant inventor figured out a way to more efficiently turn the omelet mixture over by creating a pan hinged in the middle with a separate "flipping" section. All of a sudden, every person who wants to make an omelet has an easier way of doing it—with a very simple solution, I might add!

Advice from the Pros

Every successful product fulfills a need. Start by identifying the need your product will fill and get an idea if it is a need shared by a large group of people.
—Thomas McLinden, president, Evo Design LLC

Ideas for improving existing products and services are everywhere. Perhaps there is a task you find difficult or time-consuming. Do you have an idea to make it easier, faster, or better? Look closely at the things you do in your own life. What bothers you about what exists in a particular situation—or that *doesn't exist* for that matter? Is there a problem you've encountered in those everyday menial tasks? A problem can always be solved.

Develop a *solution* to that problem with a *product* or a *service*, and before you know it, you will be on your way to success.

I like to look at product conception from three illustrative perspectives: the mousetrap, the better mousetrap, and the cheaper mousetrap. I'll explain each perspective in turn.

- *The mousetrap.* This is an entirely *new* product. The mousetrap itself was conceived by identifying a missing element in life. It was something truly innovative, with nothing else like it on the market back in the late 1800s. That original, very familiar, flat piece of wood with a spring-loaded wire for catching mice was an amazing innovation, yet to be improved upon in terms of its simple and successful technology.

For our purposes, other "mousetraps" would include products like the television, the hula hoop, even the Pet Rock, or the CD player. Also, The Segway Human Transporter or even the Universal Gym weight machine (the first weight-training machine) would fit here. However, there are very few "new" products that get introduced through infomercials. Most products are improvements on existing products that feature new technologies combined with or added to them. Which brings us to . . .

- *The better mousetrap.*   This is something we've all seen before, only now it works better than it used to—simply put, it is something that is "new and improved." In the world of mousetraps, this might be the larger mousetrap that holds several regular mousetraps and is built to capture several mice at once, or the electronic mouse zapper made to keep the mice away altogether.

Infomercial marketing doesn't just focus on "better" in a comparative sense; it focuses on value, convenience, or something that makes your life easier; it focuses on the new-technology aspect, as opposed to the "simply-better" aspect. The "better mousetrap" encompasses a great many products seen in DR marketing (infomercials). Products such as the Edgemaster or the EverLife Flashlight fall under this category as they're perceived as improvements upon the basic paint roller and the battery-powered flashlight, respectively. However, also included here are products like the Bikini Touch, a hair remover product that worked similarly to an earlier version of the product (the Finishing Touch, which was based upon another pre-existing product, but offered a better price to the consumer); the only difference was that the blade head was altered slightly for better results around a woman's bikini line. Other examples would be the Chef Wizard tongs, which also work as a combination spatula/whisk; the Miracle Blade, a better kitchen knife; and the Pasta Pro, an improvement upon the idea of a regular cooking pot.

If your product fits in this category of "better," then you likely have a concept or improvement on a product that has a high likelihood of success in DR marketing. But understand that it is still not definite that your product is right for DR marketing. You need to look further still; you need to look at your "unique selling proposition" (USP, which I will discuss later in this chapter). Your USP alone should be enough to sell via this format and make your product a standout. This is something that requires a more detailed understanding, and we will further discuss this and other important criteria in evaluating whether your item is right for TV later in this chapter. But, for now, if your idea is for an improved product or new technology added to an existing product, you're one step closer to achieving your success.

Advice from the Pros

Research products similar to yours. Review where they faulted and where they have succeeded.
—Jason Falk, Product Designer, Tank Industries

- *The cheaper mousetrap.* This is the third perspective of product conception. What happens here is that you identify a product within a category that is strong—the product sells well and many people have an item from the category. You determine a way to make something within that category cheaper and accessible to even more people.

In our mousetrap example this would be to take the spring-loaded board trap and use less expensive material—perhaps a cheaper wood base, a weaker spring and thinner piece of metal wire, or something else. The glue trap is another example that is less expensive than the standard board-and-spring mousetrap. The goal of the cheaper mousetrap is to make something more affordable—it will appeal to the public because of its lower price, but it will also have to accomplish the same function (maybe not as well, but certainly effectively enough). Keep in mind that this does not mean your product is "cheap"; it just means that it is less expensive than the similar product already on the market. Sometimes "more" is not better.

Many products have a more expensive predecessor; we see many products sold in a high-end store for $100 and then similar products sold at mass-market stores for $30 not because the stores sell them for less but because they are made of less expensive materials—plastic casing instead of steel or aluminum, for example. The plastic product may not necessarily last as long or even work as well as the steel product, but as long as it satisfies the need, accomplishes the task at hand, and serves many people well, it too can be successful, and in some cases even more so.

Many household items and hardware products are great examples of these types of items. Blenders, toasters, waffle makers, wrenches, hammers, electric screwdrivers, laser levels, and so on—we have all seen them, these commercial-grade examples used by the pros that become available with polished steel or aluminum outer casings and stainless-steel blades in the high-end department stores or specialty catalogs, only to be found later in the discount stores with plastic casings, weaker motors, and lesser-quality steel blades. But these lesser materials do not mean these products aren't good; professional contractors and master chefs require more precision and durability from their tools than do the average consumers. For the consumer, sometimes cheaper *is* better, and you might very well be the one who has the idea on how to achieve that.

The laser line level is another perfect example of a product that was initially too expensive for the average consumer but that was subsequently constructed in a less costly way and ultimately made its way to DR television. Originally, the professional laser line level unit sold for nearly $200, but then a consumer version was eventually brought to market for $60. Finally, with some manufacturing ingenuity, a direct marketing company was able to develop and bring to market the Laser-Straight for just $19.95, and it was of great quality, and it was perfect for general household use. Amazing? No, this was simply the result of identifying a way to create an existing product at a lower cost, while still meeting the standards of most consumers. The key was preserving the aspects of the product that are vital to consumers' needs while finding a way to offer it to the masses at a price that made sense.

Summary: The "new" mousetrap—an innovation in catching mice, where a metal rod snapped down and trapped mice—was actually a *new* technology. Though great for capturing an entire new consumer market, "new" is not necessarily best approached via infomercial marketing.

The "better" mousetraps were the ones that could catch six at a time and featured higher-grade materials and improved technology. The "better" is good when introducing a better or improved technology within a proven category. This format works well for DR marketing, and many products "as seen on TV" fall into this category.

The third mousetrap, the "cheaper" product version, may have been made with a pressed board platform versus the solid wood base of the original. Almost as effective but much less expensive, the "cheaper" could work well for DR marketing if the category has proven mass-appeal at an already higher price and it preserves functionality in terms of meeting the needs of the consumer.

The important thing to remember is that all three of these mousetrap concepts are great—they all work well, and success can come from all. However, it's also important to remember that not every product is appropriate for direct response marketing. There are many people with great ideas that can be very profitable, but their ideas would never sell on television. Find your category above, determine your USP, and follow that path. Now, to find out if your product concept is right for DR TV, it's time to define and develop your idea.

Your Unique Selling Proposition (USP)

Your unique selling proposition is what makes your product different from everything else out there. Essentially, it's why the consumer should buy your product instead of anyone else's, even if it may seem similar. Get the very best features of your product condensed to one brief sentence, and you've got your USP.

DEFINING AND DEVELOPING YOUR IDEA FOR TV

It is important that you understand the difference between *coming up with* an idea and *developing* that idea. Almost everyone, at some point in his or her life, has had an amazing idea for a product that could potentially enjoy tremendous success. Yet only a few people ever realize that success. The difference between those who have that success and those who don't often lies in the way they developed their ideas.

Frequently people come to me with their ideas for new products. Sometimes these ideas are tremendous, and sometimes they are not very good at all. Too many times, however, it is hard for me to judge whether an idea is good or not because the person presenting it to me has not done the background work—the "mental homework" of thinking it through on all levels.

You may have heard people use the acronym "DIY" before—it stands for "do it yourself," and it is an important and helpful concept for many entrepreneurs. I want you to remember a similar acronym essential for success in direct response marketing: DYI:

"Develop your idea." I cannot stress this enough: No matter how solid your original idea, it will go nowhere unless you define it and develop it. I have had ideas that I swore would make tremendous profits, only to learn that some small problem—some tiny area I had overlooked— was blocking my success. The problem could almost always be fixed, but not until I'd gone back to identify the problem and further develop my original concept.

Advice from the Pros

The more organized you are, the more efficient you will be in bringing your product to life, and to market. I keep a folder of all my product research—do not throw anything away EVER.

—Jason Falk, product development, Tank Industries

This happened recently with an abdominal fitness product I developed (an exercise machine for building your abs). I thought about all the aspects of the machine, worked diligently on the design, and worked with professional engineers on mechanics, but it was not until I finished my first prototype that I realized the center of gravity was off—meaning that when the users sat on my exercise machine and did the first sit-up, they would flip over backwards.

As an "expert," I was not expecting to be done at this stage, and I knew there were going to be several more stages in development for working the kinks out. The same is true for you: You need to go the distance and follow all of the steps, so you will find the problems. If you don't do this, others will find the problems for you, and your product's value will be tarnished. I have had many inventors bring me products at first-stage development thinking the product was ready to bring to market, or even ready for presentation for licensing purposes, when in reality the product still needed to go through several *more* stages of development.

The first step, therefore, in developing your idea is to get it out of your head and put the specifics clearly onto paper. This is that first step in doing the mental homework I referred to above.

To help you with this, take some quiet time to sit down and write out all of your thoughts about your product idea. As a starting point, ask yourself these questions:

1. ***What is it?*** Actually write it down. Define it first in as many words as possible and then in as few words as possible. This will help formulate the marketing and selling of your product.

2. ***How will it be better?*** What are the product advantages or design features? What are the target markets (whom are you selling it to)? What sets it apart from similar products, if there are any, already on the market? This is where you consider the USP. Basically, you're asking yourself, "What does my product do to make life easier?" You've created an affordable home gym anybody can use *any*where! You've taken all the clumsy mess out of bathing the dog! You've made it so much quicker and easier to hang a picture! What is your USP? You may even have several of them.

3. ***Why do people want or need it?*** Again let's explore the concept. Take a survey of your friends or family and ask them, "Could you use something like this? Will my product make your life easier?"

Advice from the Pros

Colors, names, materials, and size are all important features that you will want other people's opinions on. Make sure the people you talk to are well diversified with respect to gender and age. The more equipped you are with information about the demographics of your consumers, the better your product will be.

—Jason Falk, product designer, Tank Industries

4. *Is it right for TV?* When looking at a product or concept to market on TV, you must look at a few key factors. Does your product appeal to the masses, and is it demonstrable? Those are two important factors, and there are a few more. We'll talk about all of them in detail in later chapters on the different types of DR marketing campaigns.

By now, having gone through this chapter and having formulated your concept—if not on paper then in your mind—you should be ready to make your first pencil drawing. This is the first visual look at your idea, and it will be your first step toward making the prototype, that is, a working model, of your creation.

Do you have a clear image of your product now—that is, how it looks to you, how it works for others, and how it will be marketed? If so, you should be getting excited. You know your product, understand its benefits, your friends and family love it, and you believe everyone wants or needs it. So let's move on—time to make your product idea a reality!

Direct Response Marketing Success Story

Inspiration at Kmart—Coming Up with a Concept

Many times, great ideas just come to us when we least expect them. Other times we have work for them. One of my very first product ideas was like that; I had to work to find it.

My children were very young at the time; this is in the early 1990s, and I knew I wanted to develop a product for the children's market, but I literally had no idea what that product would be. I knew products with Power Rangers, Looney Tunes, Rugrats, and various other licensed properties were hot categories, but I had no experience in that area and couldn't come up with a way to enter the market, that I knew I wanted to be in.

Well, there I was in Kmart, walking up and down the aisles looking at every product on the shelves, knowing I wanted to find some-

(continued)

thing that would make a great children's product depicting these licensed characters. But it had to be something new, innovative—something that wasn't already out there. I had walked back and forth for some time, coming up with nothing when, suddenly, there it was—brown paper lunch bags!

That's right, lunch bags. Every kid takes lunch in them, every household uses them, but they are plain and brown and boring. What if I could print on them the characters kids like and give parents an exciting alternative to lunch boxes? Great idea!! And I did it, and we sold over 10 million bags in our first year and a half.

Lesson: Sometimes you have to work for your idea.

KEY CONCEPTS TO REMEMBER

1. The best ideas come from those things you are involved with. Think about the kids, hobbies, work, chores, school, and so on.

2. When inventing for your first time, stay within those areas you are familiar with.

3. Look for problems that you encounter in your everyday life.

4. Define your idea:

   a. Is it entirely new?

   b. Is it an improvement over something that already exists?

   c. Or is it a less expensive version of something that already exists?

5. DYI: Develop your idea—develop the concept thoroughly, take your time, and think it through.

6. Define your USP: your unique selling proposition.

2

Developing an Appropriate Idea

You've gotten your concept out of your head and onto paper. You have considered a variety of different facets when it comes to developing your idea. Friends and family have all told you they could use your product. But one big question remains: Is it right for DR TV? Will you move ahead and say to yourself, "This is my MOST—My One Simple Thing!"

It might turn out to be that MOST, but you must consider a simple fact: Some ideas just aren't right for the direct response (DR) market. The plasma television, for instance. Sure, now it's a popular product, but DR TV would have been the wrong venue for its introduction; besides its high price, you cannot truly show its features, or even its best feature—the picture quality—because the average TV won't capture the clear picture of plasma. And to demonstrate how a plasma TV works, all you do is turn it on and watch a picture, which means there isn't much to demonstrate to the TV viewers. Although you can show its slimness, that feature alone won't capture a viewer's attention to the extent that he or she will order the product by phone because the viewer cannot truly experience the picture quality. Furthermore, the original high price of plasmas would have made the purchase too much of a buying risk to the customer than would, say, a fat-reducing chicken griller, hair remover product, or even a singing fish, at a much lower price point.

With plasma's current popularity and recent price reductions, and thus mass-market familiarity, an inexpensive version of the plasma with a quality guarantee might work in DR, but as you have seen, the category has been one of traditional advertising, driving potential customers to the stores to view and experience the product for themselves.

When considering whether your product is right for TV, there are several key questions you need to ask:

1. ***Does your invention solve a problem?*** Particularly when selling on TV, you want to make sure your product ***solves a common, understandable problem***. The problem is your ***hook***—the essential thing that will make people want your product. The bigger the problem it solves, the more desirable the product. ***But remember***, many people may not even know they have this "problem" until you point it out to them. Remember my lunch bags story in Chapter 1? The only "problem" I solved was how to make the kids a little happier at lunchtime (thus, not great for DR TV). Get creative and determine what kind of problem ***your*** product solves.

2. ***Is it easy to use?*** The simpler, the better. If your product is difficult to use, people will not like it. They might try it and send it back, or they might give up on it before they use it, or they may not even buy it because it sounds too complicated. Remember, people want ***convenience***, to be able to do things better or faster.

3. ***Can everyone use your item? Does every household need one?*** Think in terms of mass appeal. The larger your target audience, the better your chance of success on TV. If your product appeals to only a small group of people, it is considered a product for a ***niche market***. Niche products can do

very well, and a niche can actually be a very large group. Take, for example, men who are balding—a relatively large group but still considered a niche compared to, say, all the men between the ages of 18 and 60. When marketing on TV, you want to *target the largest, broadest group possible*. For example, "all households" or "all men over 18" or "all women over 18" or, ideally, "everyone." Remember, the larger your audience, the better chance of success.

Advice from the Pros

A product that addresses a very specific niche may not sell enough to be successful, even if it is purchased by a large percentage of the target audience. On the other hand, a product that has a universal appeal if purchased by even a small percentage of the target audience could be a big success. A product for hot air balloon pilots will likely sell a lot less than a product for people who drive cars.

—Thomas McLinden, president, Evo Design LLC

4. *Is the product easy to explain or, more importantly, to demonstrate?* This is an important aspect, one of the key factors that grabs the viewer's attention and gets them to watch. If your demonstration (or "demo") has a real "Wow!" factor, it can make your product a success.

Think of the original Ginsu knives—the "Wow!" was that it cut through a tin can and then sliced a tomato in the air with one quick pass of the knife—Wow! If your product is easy to use but hard to explain, your customer may not understand it and lose interest. By the same token, if you can easily show how your product works but it does *not* have the "Wow!" factor, they might not perceive a need to buy your product. Even a novelty product like the Boogie Bass worked on TV simply because of the "Wow"—the fish jumping up and actually singing.

Carefully formulate and think about the idea for your product. Think about the ways it could be demonstrated and if it will provide your audience with a "Wow!"

5. ***Can you offer your item at a good price?*** You don't have to know the answer yet. It is more important to follow your dream of realizing the product and sometimes let the marketplace determine the cost or selling price. The key to offering a "good" price is not always making it as cheap as possible but to have a relatively low manufacturing cost and a high perceived value (more on this later). If you convey to the consumer that your product is a bargain at twice the price (the perceived value), you will always turn a profit.

6. ***Does your product appeal visually to the intended user?*** Will your product cause a channel surfer to stop and watch? Whenever possible, you want your product to ***look good***. This doesn't mean it has to be pretty or even colorful necessarily but that there must be something about it to make the viewer want to see more. Think about the infomercials and DR advertisements you've watched before—what made you pay attention to those products?

Advice from the Pros

People don't always want cheap. People want a fair price for quality.
—Ron Popeil

Some of the answers to these questions may be hard to determine just now. That's okay. As you move along in development, the answers will present themselves.

If your product does fit the criteria above, you are on your way

Advice from the Pros

One word of advice to the first-time inventor? *Patience.*

—Jason Falk, product designer, Tank Industries

to creating a successful DR TV item. If your concept meets some but not all of these criteria, that's okay too. You might face more hurdles, and you may have a tougher sell, but believe in yourself and you will overcome. (In later chapters, we will explore several other avenues outside of DR TV for bringing your product to market.)

But now you do know and understand the criteria for DR marketing. You have asked yourself the six questions and understand the basic product criteria for DR marketing; you have refined your product concept; and you are ready to begin the journey as we move forward to the next chapter, where we'll talk about developing a prototype.

So let's jump in and *keep moving . . .*

Direct Response Marketing Success Story

The Recent College Graduate and the Fishing Lure— Developing Your Idea

About a year ago a young college graduate was referred to me for a product he had developed. The key here was the use of the word "developed." The reality was that he had only conceptualized the product and drawn it out on paper. It was a good thought but he had no patents, no intellectual property protection, and most importantly, no research on the category. The product was not "developed," and that was the problem.

(continued)

A concept is really worthless by itself because its function cannot be substantiated, and the market for it has not been proven yet to exist, So at this stage, it cannot be sold to a consumer because there is nothing to sell.

However, this college student had great energy and a great belief in his concept. After speaking with him for a while, I explained to him how to add value. He then took his concept to the next level. He researched the market and was able to gain enough information and insights to have a prototype made. From the prototype, he was able to do two things:

1. Prove the viability of his product (that is, "Does it work?").

2. Present a working product to possible investors, marketers, and other people with a potential interest.

By fully developing his idea into a working product, he was able to move forward. He has recently sold the product to QVC; and he is negotiating with an infomercial marketing company to license his product.

Lesson: Take your concept and *fully* develop it.

KEY CONCEPTS TO REMEMBER

1. Can everyone use your item? Does every household need one?

2. Does your invention solve a problem?

3. Is it easy to use?

4. Is the product easy to explain and, more importantly, to demonstrate?

5. Can you offer your item at a good price? (Does your product have a high perceived value?)

6. Does your product appeal visually to the intended user?

3

The Prototype

Designing, Developing, and
Testing Your First Prototype

IT'S TIME TO MAKE YOUR PRODUCT

My One Simple Thing—that is, your MOST. Now that you have it, what do you do with it?

The idea stage has passed, and you need to go into the reality stage. You need to ensure that your idea actually works, actually functions, and can do what you think it can. But how do you establish that? Start by asking yourself some questions including these: How do I make it a reality? How do I make a working sample? Where do I go? Whom do I see? And, perhaps most important, whom can I trust? After all, this is *my* big idea, *my* MOST.

The best way to protect it and ensure that this great idea will never be stolen is simple: Write it down and lock it up in a drawer, and *never open up that drawer again.* You will have nothing to fear, and your product will never be stolen. Of course, it will also never be developed.

To convert your idea into reality, you need to let go of the fears that someone will steal your idea. Of course, anything is possible, and that's why there are methods available to you to protect your idea even in its beginning stages of development. We'll discuss those methods more thoroughly in the next chapter. But you can start the development process without worrying too much about someone's stealing your idea at this point. Then as you go along in the development process, you can add the protections your need. For now, trust other people. So let's look at how you can get out of the idea stage and into reality.

PUTTING YOUR IDEA ON PAPER

A great way to help you visualize your idea is to simply draw it. Don't worry if you're not an artist or if you don't know one end of a pencil from the other. Just draw a stick figure or a basic line drawing—any scribble that *you* can interpret. Draw something that helps you *see* the product out of your head and down on paper, which is the key at this point.

Draw it big, draw it small. Don't like how it looks? It's not what you envisioned? Not a problem; draw it again. Just keep at it until you have something you feel you can interact with, analyze, and consider (and reconsider, and *re*-reconsider). Don't worry about scale or dimension; just indicate size and details with arrows or words. The drawing is simply something to help you visualize the aesthetics of your product and to get that dialogue going, even if the only person you're talking to is yourself.

Advice from the Pros

From Thomas Edison to Richard Dyson, many famous inventors were also tinkerers. The best way to prove an idea is to make a working model. Most people would be surprised to learn that many sophisticated products started out as very crude models.
—Thomas McLinden, president, Evo Design LLC

Your creation has begun. You are an inventor! With something to look at, you'll be able to determine whether anyone else is looking at something like it somewhere else. That's right; your product may already exist. It happens. It has happened to me, and it may happen to you. But don't be deterred.

Go online; that's our best source of getting lots of information—visually and textually—fast these days. Head to a search engine; any will do. It can be Lycos.com, MSN.com, Dogpile.com, Google, or any other. All you need to do is type in words that relate to your product, read descriptions of what you find, and look for other words that relate to your product. For instance, if you've invented a new product to open cans, type in "can openers," "electric can openers," "kitchen utensils," "can openers in history," or perhaps even "corkscrews." Your purpose in running these searches is to be certain that nobody else has hit upon your idea (and so you want to cover every avenue possible) or if someone has, that his or her implementation of it is recognizably different from yours—either in its approach (functionality) or design.

Advice from the Pros

After coming up with your idea, the very first step is to conduct a market search to determine whether the idea is novel.

—Peter D. Murray, Esq., intellectual property (IP) attorney, Cooper & Dunham LLP

The listed portal sites above are good resources because those in particular allow you to search either text or images. On any of those sites, if you type in "can opener," you will get pages and pages of text about them, selling them, and the history of them. Click the "images" link, and you can see what they all look like.

Don't let this task overwhelm you. Give yourself a reasonable allotted time. Maybe an hour or two at most for simple ideas and maybe longer for more complicated ideas or subtle improvements. If you're still sitting at the computer three days after your initial search, you just may have gone too far. But take in as much information as you can from the search because you will also learn about the category and overall market through the process. Once you get to a certain point in your search and have gathered much in the way of market information, you will want to explore the legal (patent) side of your product—but that's for later. We'll go into intellectual property (IP) and patent searches in Chapter 4, and those searches are more thorough.

What happens when you do an Internet search and you find a similar product? Now what? Throw it all away? Scrap this idea and move on? Never! *Keep moving.*

 ## Direct Response Marketing Success Story

The Over Easy Flip Pan—Overcoming the "Similar-Product" Hurdle

I had noticed that in the category of cooking, the products that offered an ability to flip eggs, pancakes, and food in general were very popular. There were all kinds of items on the market like the Grip & Flip spatula and the Kitchen Wizard spatula, the Flipping Omelet Pan and the Perfect Pancake maker. I was watching the Food Network one night and watched with amazement as the chef easily sautéed and flipped the food he was cooking. We have probably all seen professional chefs accomplish this feat many times.

That's when it hit me; there must be a way for someone as untalented in the kitchen as I am to flip food like that. So I started on the journey to invent something that would make that possible, and I began by doing some research on the Internet and conducting a preliminary patent search. The patent search I did on my own just by visiting the USPTO.gov Web site. Unfortunately, although other Web

(continued)

sites on the Internet did not show much in terms of what I wanted, the USPTO Web site did. There was already a patent that had been granted for a pan for sautéing food.

But I didn't let this discovery deter me. Instead, I studied the patent. After reading the description provided, I realized that the patented product covered only part of what I wanted to do. So at that point I turned to a pro—my patent attorney—to make sure that I was interpreting what I was reading properly. What we found was that I was correct and that I could develop a pan that "flipped" food, as opposed to sautéing it. I just had to alter the shape of my pan, which I could do based on an expired patent (see Chapter 4 for more details on patents). And so I did, developing the "Over Easy Flip Pan." Within months after development, we were able to sell our product in Walgreens, and we were on our way.

Lesson: Don't let obstacles stop you from moving forward. Look at them as challenges and opportunities to better develop your product.

Study this similar (or same) item. Look at how it was constructed, what materials it's made from, and how it works. Are there others like it? Have others that exist borrowed on the same idea but taken it in a new direction? What are these competing products like? Look through everything you can find. It's very possible your idea is different in some very small, yet important, way—a way that might improve on what exists. Or, possibly, you may find yourself inspired with a *brand-new* way to differentiate your idea. After all, the person who created the color television did not create the television. One small thing can, in itself, be a million-dollar "new idea."

Advice from the Pros

Even the most novel idea can share some parts with existing products in order to make a first mock-up.
—Thomas McLinden, president, Evo Design LLC

IS IT AN ORIGINAL IDEA?

It is also a possibility that your product's application—that is, the way in which and/or the purpose *for* which it may be used—will differ drastically. There are circumstances in which that too may be an advantage (again, we'll get into this kind of detail in the next chapter).

If you have indeed found something similar, you may want to go jump ahead to Chapter 4 and then return to this chapter when your information search has yielded the results you need.

Worst case? You may have to reinvent, or even completely reimagine, your idea. Try to stay in familiar territory, but do not give up.

But let's assume the Internet has elicited positive results, and you can't find anything that is exactly like your product. Your stick drawing is calling to you. What now? You have to ask yourself a few questions. First, will it function? If you believe it will, the obvious next question is, how? Think of the mechanics of your product. Again, don't worry if you don't know whether ball bearings or a pulley system is best, or even if you don't know the difference between the two. Just know that something needs to move (or light up, or click, or whistle, or do something else), and at some point you will find out *how* to make that part do what it needs to do. At the stage of finding *how,* you will then seek out someone to help get your concept into a form that is easy for you, and others, to understand.

Checklist

Questions to Ask at the Development Stage

1. Is my idea new or an improvement on an existing idea?
2. Will it function?
3. How will it function?

Costs Pyramid

Design Firms: The *peak* of perfection: more likely to have experience presenting and working with manufacturers and/or licensors.

Freelance Graphic Designers: Will probably give you more personal attention; may have personal experience with manufacturers and other commercial firms.

Teachers: Close, personal attention, but teaching is very time consuming work; may not have the time and dedication you need.

Students: *Lowest* cost; a very possible lack of experience and professionalism; real-world business experience not likely.

Experience Pyramid

Figure 3–1   Cost and experience pyramid for design phase.

How? Well, you will need an artist, a professional (see Figure 3–1). Assuming you are not one (I certainly am not), there are several options, each of varying costs, that you can pursue.

Initially, you can go to a design firm. This is likely your most expensive option, but you can be assured of getting a professionally rendered artistic interpretation of your product. Find design firms in your local business directory or on the Internet.

Another option is to go to a professional graphic designer who will work with you on a freelance (or work-for-hire) basis. A graphic designer usually has some basic knowledge, if not advanced, on engineering details that may be relevant to your concept. The cost here will vary depending on the amount of experience the artist has and the complexity of your product, but overall an independent or freelance artist is more economical to hire than is a design firm. Also, in many cases a design firm may even hire the same independent artist you might find, and the firm will just add to the fee it charges you an extra fee for its handling of the project. But it is important to note that even in that scenario, there are added values from the design firm to you—its exposure, expertise, and knowledge are generally very broad, and the firm can sometimes suggest changes and modifications to both your product and its marketing. That value add-on can easily outweigh the out-of-pocket costs to you. At this stage, though, base your decision on your needs and the budget you have established.

If you want to find a freelancer to work directly with, ask friends if they know of anyone who could take such an assignment or check the Internet for possibilities. Freelancers often have their own Web sites; search "[your hometown or nearest city] + graphic designer" at any search site.

The most cost efficient route would be to go to a local college, high school, or even a design or technical school. There you can ask teachers or students to help out. In many cases students will work for free, just happy to have something in their portfolio, or you can give them a small stipend and make them doubly happy.

Advice from the Pros

It is very difficult to proceed without professional drawings. We refer to these as *control art*.
—Jason Falk, product designer, Tank Industries

Whichever you choose, *do not be afraid to share your idea.* There are simple ways to present and protect your idea through *Nondisclosure Agreements* (or *NDAs*), but again, we'll talk further about this, and patent protection as well, in Chapter 4. For now, know that most people are just happy, even excited, to help. People love to be part of something new; they love to hear themselves talk, love to offer advice, and feel important. The very fact that you've asked that person to help you will be exciting for them.

CREATING A PROTOTYPE

Whichever option you have chosen for the artistic interpretation of your item, the next step will be to get a *prototype* made. This is a word people hear a lot, yet most don't know exactly what it means. A prototype isn't always that perfect-looking "car of the future" at the auto show. It can be a rough estimate, or an approximation, of what your idea will look like.

Whether it is a rough approximation or exactly what you feel the final product should look like, the purpose remains the same: You want to be able to show by example what your product does. (Who are you trying to show that to? The answer for now is none other than *you*. I'll explain below.) You also want to answer that all-important question: Will it work? You don't have to worry about the mechanics; they may change. For the electronics, electric parts, lenses, readouts—all of that comes out in the engineering phase.

The prototype is also called your *breadboard,* which is a basic form of your product or device that will simulate the task, movement, or general functionality of the product. Once you have that first prototype, you can try it out and analyze your product even further. Just as you had a simple drawing at the start to interact with and utilize as you moved to the next stage, you will now have an actual three-dimensional form of your product that you might be able to truly use. And if you can't, that's okay too; this is all about form and the *possibility* of functionality. Either way, you'll have opportunity to better determine the viability of your idea and decide if something needs to be tweaked. (More of which we will explore when we reach the engineering phase of the development process.)

Advice from the Pros

Do not take shortcuts in the prototype phase—it will only lead to unforeseen problems and costs.
—Jason Falk, product designer, Tank Industries

Costs Pyramid

Prototype Companies or Mechanical Engineering Firms: They are at the apex, the peak, of their game, knowing exactly the materials and the engineering necessities of virtually any project you put in front of them; they also have the real-world business experience that can be crucial at this stage. Firms may be less personal. This level often expects to call the shots and, depending on your personality, could possibly not be what you're looking for. Costs will certainly be high.

Local Mechanics, Artists, or Builders: You can find the know-how, but the real-world business interaction could be hit-or-miss.

Teachers and/or Professors: This is more of a luck-of-the-draw. Some teachers make it their business to keep their feet in the water and keep themselves sharp; others have taken to focusing on the curriculum of their teaching schedule.

Students: Real-world experience is very unlikely, and the know-how is, perhaps obviously, still being developed.

Experience Pyramid

Figure 3–2   Cost and experience pyramid for prototype development phase.

As it was with the drawing, you may need a pro for the task of creating a prototype as well. Before you divulge what your project is, determine if the person you approach can truly help. Depending on your product, you may have to turn to a mechanical engineer, a sculptor, a car mechanic, a cabinetmaker, metallurgist, or even computer programmer—or perhaps a combination of those. As with the graphic artist, there are people with different levels of experience and know-how—each of whom have their pros and cons in their professional capacities (see Figure 3–2).

Advice from the Pros

A rough mock-up can often be made by a carpenter, mechanic, or someone else who has a mechanical aptitude. Even a crude model can be a great tool for communicating your idea to others.
—Thomas McLinden, president, Evo Design LLC

One very important point about your prototype that you must keep in mind is that just because you envision your final product to be made of plastic or metal, that does not mean you can't create an approximation of it in wood or even with household products found at an office supply store (see the direct response marketing success stories later in this chapter) or a junkyard for that matter.

Direct Response Marketing Success Story

The StikiBoard: Developing Your Prototype

I wanted to create a board that worked similarly to a sticky note but that worked the other way: One could post any piece of paper onto it because it would be coated with a light adhesive material (no Post-it notes required). Your youngest drew a terrific picture? A family photo makes you smile? Need to remind you-know-who to take out the trash? You could put any and all of it on the StikiBoard without using thumbtacks, pins, or tape. And, even better, anything you put up could also come down without damaging your pictures, photos, laundry lists, or what-have-you.

It was a great idea. I was excited!

I went to an art supply store and found the materials I needed. Plain board, something I could use to make the board adhesive, and a narrow plastic frame that I could use to show that it could be decorative as well as useful. And some other miscellaneous items to help get my point across.

Soon, I had my prototype, and all at very low cost. It was enough to be able to set up meetings and garner interest in the product. I even produced a short-form commercial for the product based on initial response. Yet, despite the interest and the commercial, this particular project did not move forward. But because of my ability to create a prototype from existing materials, I was able to find out quickly and relatively inexpensively that this product was not "the one."

Lessons:

1. Believe in your product, no matter what. Not every idea is a success, but you can learn from your experience nevertheless.

(*continued*)

2. Make "friends" with your environment. The art supply store provided me with an inexpensive approach to make my prototype as well as a number of avenues to explore for the look and practical construction of my item.

Another important thing is that you shouldn't get frustrated if the prototype isn't what you had hoped because that is what this stage is for. Discover your issues and problems now, and work out the flaws. Maybe the person or company who helped you make it didn't quite hit the mark, perhaps because of your description or the way they interpreted what you said. If that's the case, don't get frustrated. Try to figure out where the communication broke down. Always keep communication open; you'll find that in-person and phone conversations will work better than e-mails. (This is a valuable tip that you will want to remember at *every* stage of this process. Never underestimate the power of vocal persuasion.) Tone and inflection can convey some ideas much better than written words, and if there's a question, the person you're talking to can ask it right then and there—leaving less chance for his or her having to make possibly incorrect assumptions about your intentions. Maybe the engineer made it exactly to your specs, but it still doesn't work quite right. That's okay too. This is exactly what a prototype is for; it's an opportunity to work out the kinks. Your "engineer" may have suggestions to fix these things, often before the work is finished.

Never underestimate the input of the people you're working with because that input is exactly the reason you approached them. As a matter of fact, you shouldn't overlook *any* of your resources. I've shown products to my kids, and with their young, wide-eyed innocent point of view, they have opened my eyes to aspects I had completely missed.

Direct Response Marketing Success Story

The Bun and Thigh Express: The Value of the Input of Others

My big idea would make Suzanne Somers appear an amateur: A home workout machine that exercised the thighs and buttocks by replicating the motion of a squat. And, much like adding weights to a barbell at the gym, you could adjust the tension for a harder workout.

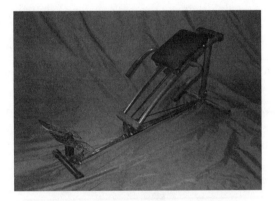

Figure 3–3   Second round prototype.

Figure 3–4   Final product rendering.

(*continued*)

When I was fully prepared, I went to the gym and watched a friend do a couple of free-weight squats, looking at the posture, positioning, and the angle in which he moved. This provided me with the basis of how my *machine* had to look and move.

The materials chosen for the prototype by the design firm I was using were basic. They used a cushion from a chair, wheels from an inline skate, and a wooden base.

Then we tested it; but it didn't feel quite right yet.

Back to the gym.

This time with the designer. He realized we had missed a key issue: the angle at which the body moved when doing a squat correctly. This would determine the angle of the chair and how it was held on the base.

Back to the prototype.

We tested it again and again, making minor adjustments until it did exactly what I originally set out for it do and more importantly, what it was supposed to do. (See Figures 3–3 and 3–4.)

Lesson: Test and retest; don't be afraid to make changes or reimagine your original concept when necessary. And listen to the input of those helping you with your design—third-party input is invaluable.

Advice from the Pros

The real world does not take into account emotions when it comes to your product. Separate emotional desire, and put on your business head.

—Barbara Tulipane, president and CEO, Electronic Retailing Association

Use your prototype. Even if it's not exactly what your product will be in terms of materials or it's not fully functional, it should be a close enough approximation to allow you to test aspects of it. Is the size okay? Will the pieces work together? Is the material used for this prototype better or worse than what you had envisioned? Is it structurally sound? Play with the prototype, and ruminate on all the positives and the negatives. This isn't a race. There is no need to rush through any phase of the creation. And a slow, careful study of your prototype could save you money, time, and many headaches as you move to either presenting your product or creating an improved prototype.

The processes in this chapter will allow you to become more and more familiar with your invention and the needs of those consumers you want to sell it to. You have gathered further information from the Web, you know which kinds of experts—a welder or an engineer for instance—will be able to help create a prototype. You've studied similar products, and you have looked into possible resources for the building of your breadboard. And this is just the beginning.

You will probably discover more questions, and you may need help in finding the answers. But again, do not be concerned. This is all part and parcel of the creative process. Just remember, don't let that momentum go. *Keep moving . . .*

 Direct Response Marketing Success Story

From the Mouths of Babes: The Power of Using All Your Resources

I was helping a client of mine develop a hairbrush that rotated on its handle, a spinning hairbrush to be more precise. But we had encountered a problem; there was a patent existing for a similar item, and my client's concept would have infringed on that patent. So the assignment began.

I needed to help my client further develop the product so it would not infringe on the already existing patent. We had our brainstorming session, spoke with their patent attorney, and threw ideas back and forth all day, but no luck. Then it happened. My daughter, all of nine years old, came over to ask what I was working on. So I

(continued)

showed her the pictures from the patent while at the same time explaining the dilemma. She looked at the drawings, looked at what I was doing, and within seconds, yes, seconds, asked the question, "Why can't you just . . ."

It was that "why can't" that did it! Her viewpoint was something that we had not considered. We just never saw it. I looked and looked again. I then drew the modification she had explained, and I presented it the next day to my client and their attorney, and it worked. It wasn't the complete solution, but it put us on a path that got us to our final product and into production.

Lesson: Be open to listening to those around you—sometimes you can be too close to something to see what's there or what's not. Solutions and creative ideas are all around you. Don't allow yourself to get stuck. *Keep moving . . .*

Whether it's the artist you've worked with, a friend you trust, or the person who'll help build your prototype, listen to what people have to say about your product. Do they love it? Why? Do they think it's a waste of your time? Find out the "why" on that too! Learn from them, ask questions, let them tell you everything they think and feel. You can only benefit. And if the feedback is negative, do not, under any circumstances, let that deter you. Instead, let it propel you; let it help you make your product better! *Keep Moving . . .*

KEY CONCEPTS TO REMEMBER

1. Visualize your idea, make it a reality on paper. Simply draw it. And draw it simply.

2. Do not worry about scale or dimension. Indicate size and other details in writing.

3. Do your research. Use any online search engine to verify that your idea is unique and different.

4. Study what you find. Ask, what are they like? How are they different? Are they different? Is mine better? How is mine better?

5. Ask yourself about your product: Will it function? How will it function?

6. Hire a design firm or freelance graphic artist to take you to the next level.

7. A *prototype* is a rough estimate or approximation of what your idea will look like.

8. You will need a prototype to determine the will-it-work aspects of your development.

9. Take your time with the prototype. Do not take shortcuts.

10. Believe in your product, and make "friends" with your environment. Test and retest your prototype. Be open to changes, and listen—really listen—to those around you.

4

Legal Advice

Protecting the Idea and Yourself

Every product requires different levels of protection at different stages of its development. At times this protection is as simple as designating the information you share with others as "confidential." It is possible, of course, that you will have to consider other legal issues with your product such as safety, patent protection, or licensing.

I'll go over the basics, but ultimately the best option for you is to always consult a lawyer knowledgeable on the subject. It is also a good idea to meet with a lawyer for the purpose of determining whether your product might be also protected as a trademark, trade dress, or even copyrighted material. Specifically, you want to look for a good patent attorney (also referred to as *intellectual property* (IP) *attorneys*). Certainly if you have a friend or family member who is an attorney, you can go to that person for the basics, but if intellectual property isn't his or her specialty, he or she might miss something important in your situation. Your friend may know some of the facts, but you should still consider going to someone who *specializes* in intellectual property law, which includes trademarks, trade dress, copyright, and even such issues as unfair competition (see the details below regarding NDAs). After all, you probably wouldn't go to the local seafood restaurant for the best burger in town.

Advice from the Pros

Once a person has conceived an idea and put it into a tangible format, the first step should be to speak with an intellectual property attorney.

—Jason M. Drangel, Esq., IP attorney, Epstein Drangel Bazerman & James LLP

So let's get started with the basics. At this point, you are likely paranoid to the point that you don't even want to share your product idea with your dog. So before you begin sharing it with other people, you need to draft an agreement that stipulates that they must not talk to others about it. This agreement is referred to as a *non-disclosure agreement* (NDA), as mentioned earlier.

THE NON-DISCLOSURE AGREEMENT (NDA)

The *non-disclosure agreement* (NDA) is also called the *confidentiality agreement*, and it is used in all types of business across many platforms. Used by individual inventors and large multinational corporations alike, it's simply the most common way to protect oneself when sharing information. An NDA states that any original thoughts or ideas you share will remain private. It explains that the person you're sharing your ideas with is hearing these ideas *solely* to help you with your project. In other words, he or she cannot legally bring the idea to someone else, cannot claim the idea as his or her own, and cannot share the information outside of the parameters covered by the agreement.

Advice from the Pros

For the developer of the idea, the NDA or confidentiality agreement should always be signed *before* the idea is disclosed.

—Peter D. Murray, Esq., IP attorney, Cooper & Dunham LLP

There are various formats of the NDA, and there are many aspects unique to a particular product, but the common purpose of all NDAs is to protect original ideas (see Figure 4–1). You want to share your idea with the understanding that those you share it with will not (1) tell others anything about it or (2) try and take the concept and develop it themselves.

The second aspect would fall under a provision generally referred to as the *noncompete clause* that states the acknowledging parties cannot work on or be involved with a *similar-functioning item* that would compete on the market with yours, nor can they give any information regarding your invention to a production or manufacturing company. For instance, if you are the creator of the Xbox, the person you have hired to help build or somehow develop your system cannot then go and create another gaming system such as the PS2 and bring that to market or work for a company that makes a competing gaming system such as the PS2.

Some details vary in these agreements, often related to geographical and/or durational limits in the noncompete clauses. And that is why we have lawyers—well, it's at least one reason. But the gist of these agreements holds: The parties to the agreement can't share the information, any information, that you provide without your permission (see the box titled "Main Points of the NDA").

Schedule A:
Developed Products and/or Product Concepts

Note: This agreement is for illustration purposes only. Please consult your attorney to determine if this form meets your individual or corporate needs.

THIS AGREEMENT is entered into between _____ ("Company") and Product Strategies, Inc., having its place of business at _____ _____ ("Recipient") so that Recipient may evaluate certain confidential and proprietary information ("Information") given it by Company that relates to the products identified in Schedule A below ("Products") with a view toward Recipient's handling aspects of the marketing and distribution and any related aspects thereof on behalf of, or in conjunction with, Company.

We (Company) have already disclosed to you and are willing to continue to disclose to you Information relating to such Products under conditions of confidentiality. The Information may be in any form, without limitation, including data, know-how, designs, specifications, samples, drawings, and other material incorporating any information relating to the Products or related marketing or financial Information. The fact is that we (Recipient) are engaged in discussions, and the entire content of all discussion between us concerning any aspect of the matters referred to in this Agreement shall be considered a part of the confidential Information.

Recipient agrees that it will keep the Information confidential and not disclose it to anyone other than those of its employees who have reasonable need to see it and use it only for the purpose of evaluation and will not use the Information for any other purposes whatsoever unless expressly authorized by Company in writing. Such employees have signed such Confidentiality Agreements with Recipient so that they are bound by this Agreement (whether currently employed or not by Recipient). Failure to abide by this Confidentiality Agreement may cause financial harm to Company for which Recipient may be held responsible. Upon demand, Recipient will return all documents and other materials in its possession, custody, or control that bear or incorporate any part of the Information so supplied to Recipient, and all such material, ideas, or products remains the sole exclusive property of Company.

The obligations under this Confidentiality Agreement shall continue for a term of two (2) years from the date indicated below, provided, however, that if the parties enter into the contemplated business relationship, this Agreement shall terminate two (2) years after the business relationship terminates.

The above provisions may not apply to any of the Information that is verifiable already in Recipient's possession in writing at the time of Company's initial disclosure to Recipient, or later becomes part of the public domain through no fault of Recipient. This Agreement shall be governed by the laws of the State of New York as if fully executed and performed in New York.

This written Agreement embodies all of the understandings and obligations between the parties with respect to the subject matter hereof.

IN WITNESS WHEREOF the parties hereto have executed this Agreement.

Product Strategies, Inc.   Company:_____

_____   _____

Name: Michael Planit   Name:
Title: President   Title: President
Date: Date:

Figure 4–1   Non-disclosure and nonuse agreement.

Main Points of the NDA

- Conversations or e-mails or any other correspondence about the idea or the product remain private.

- Improvements, changes, or new design concepts that either of you come up with regarding your product remain private.

- A noncompete clause is included stating that the contractor cannot develop your product, or even a similar (competing) one, by itself or with another company or entity.

In addition, a photo or drawing of the product may be attached if necessary. And the NDA may also include details about the contractor's fees if applicable.

Some people you encounter in the early stages may get a little nervous about signing such a document. As simple as it sounds, it is, after all, a legal document. And, more than that, it is a legal document with a certain amount of "legalese," which tends to make some people nervous. The solution is to be open with people who are anxious about signing the agreement about the necessity for it. Explain to them that it's just a way to protect your idea because you're excited about the prospects of this idea and the agreement is a way of alerting people who work on it that it is protected intellectual property. Most people appreciate the need for it, and an NDA is rarely an intimidating document, usually running only one-half to one-and-a-half pages long.

In the early stages of the development of their product, inventors will probably be speaking to many people about it. When my clients are in this stage of development, the first question they usually ask me on the subject of non-disclosure agreements is, "Does everyone have to sign one?" Well, the answer is that anyone with whom you are going to be specific about your product information should sign an agreement. But if you are seeking only general opinions from friends and family on your idea, speak openly and in general terms. Say things like, "If you had a product that could make it easier or faster to do X or that could solve the problem of Y, or could make it cheaper to do Z, would you buy it? What are some things you would look for in such a product? What if there were a product that could . . . ?"

Hopefully you get the idea—keep the discussion of the product or idea general, and don't give away the idea, but do your research and get the information you need from others. This will avoid the stress that comes with the legal part of the creative process. Even at this level of disclosure, be sure to share your information with only those people with whom you are truly comfortable and whose opinions and feedback you believe can add value to your idea.

In sum, when speaking with the people who are going to help— designers, mechanics, industry-related people, engineers, manufacturers, and others—always have them sign an NDA. In the development stages, it is very important to already have the NDA in place because its not being in place can prevent you from getting a patent at a later time. This has to do with the way information gets disseminated to the public and the way patent filings are handled. As a side note, lawyers will not need to sign an NDA as they are bound by canons (rules) of ethics and attorney-client privilege.

Advice from the Pros

NDAs should be used whenever two parties are about to enter into a relationship. The more specific the terms are about what is considered to be confidential, what the purpose of disclosure is, how the information is to be used, and for how long the information is to remain confidential, the better chance that such a document is enforceable.

    —Jason M. Drangel, Esq., IP attorney, Epstein Drangel Bazerman & James LLP

PROTECT THE IDEA

OK, so you have checked the Internet, and, after some (hopefully detailed and exhaustive) research, you have learned that you are indeed the first one with this Big Idea. This means you might even be the "first to market" with your product (an important aspect in the marketing and launch of your product). Or the converse has happened: You have found that there is someone out there, someone just like you, who noticed the need for your product or product improvement and has already marketed the idea. In other words, what inspired your creation has inspired someone else as well. What do you do? In either situation the answer is the same: It is time to find a patent (IP) attorney.

Ask friends and family first if they can recommend someone. Ask another type of attorney you may have dealt with in another situation. There are plenty of attorneys, and most everyone knows at least one—or knows someone who knows one. To help you get the ball rolling, you might want to call the local bar association for names.

Your first step in speaking with a patent attorney is to find out if you can protect your idea. If your idea is new and not "obvious" in its purpose or functionality, the answer might be yes and you will be on your way. And even if your research showed that your idea already exists in some form or another, you still may be on your way. The reason is that a patent attorney can tell you whether your product is different enough from what already exists to help you determine if it is still patentable.

When hiring an attorney, you will probably be asked to sign a retainer agreement, which indicates the terms under which you will operate with your attorney. (For an example of the type of retainer agreement a patent attorney will ask you to sign, see Appendix B.) Your patent attorney will begin with a patent search. He or she will search the U.S. Patent and Trademark Office (USPTO) records of all types to see if there is anything similar to your product or invention. You can also conduct IP searches on your own through other outlets as well. The first stop should be the Web site for the U.S. Patent and Trademark Office (www.uspto.gov). There are several other Web sites that offer this service as well, and they usually have standard fee-based packages that include a complete IP search.

The purpose of the search is not just to see if your idea has been taken already but also to check if your concept *infringes* on another person's patent. That is, someone else may have created a similar product. Sometimes that person's product may serve a different purpose or application, but it nevertheless incorporates your improvement or design idea.

Advice from the Pros

After the search has been conducted, your patent attorney will analyze the patent and determine what the scope of the patent is, whether there is an infringement, and if there is a way around the patent.
—Jason M. Drangel, Esq., IP attorney, Epstein Drangel Bazerman & James LLP

You may discover that, even though you were not aware of this when you conceived your idea, someone else has already invented it, but that person never marketed it successfully or never followed up on it properly. If that's the case or if the search results in other seemingly bad news, perhaps a similar item is patented or your item crosses into someone else's territory—do not be deterred. There are still many options open to you. For example, you can consider contacting that patent holder to discuss either forming a partnership with that person or licensing that person's patent for your needs. Your attorney can direct you in either type of situation.

Unfortunately, because this is the nature of the beast, there are times when you just have to say, "I tried, but it's been done, and I'll have to find something else." Though it certainly doesn't feel very good when it happens, remember that sometimes it is okay to walk away from one idea and move on to your next one. But before you walk, you should keep in mind that there are times—many times— when the most minor change in a single element can make a product "new"—allowing you *your own* patent or at least allowing your idea or product to stand on its own. Even if you cannot get a patent, it does not mean you should not keep going and follow my mantra of *keep moving . . .*

As an example: When developing my Over Easy Flip Pan product, as detailed in Chapter 3, I found that there already existed such a pan. But that pan was specifically for sautéing food, and it did not cover the flipping aspect of the idea. When I furthered my research, I found a patent for a pan for flipping food was already patented in 1923. The patent had long expired, and the product was in the public domain (detailed later in this chapter). Thus I was able to utilize the design. And considering that it was not an item that had been seen, as best as I could tell, for at least 80 years, I was in safe territory in regard to reintroducing it. Although I could not get a patent and although there was the sauté pan with a patent, I was still able to move forward with my product basically as I had envisioned it. An attorney specializing in patent law helped ensure that I could move forward. With the green light, I was able to secure sales within months after I began.

Of course, it is also possible that you will have to go back to the beginning and reexamine your idea. But, once again, if you do have to go back, that's okay. Remember, you're now an inventor, and you will find something else to invent. Just *keep moving . . .*

Finding out that your product doesn't conflict with—not to be confused with "compete with"—anything else on the marketplace is an important step. In fact, I cannot stress enough how much carrying out these research steps will help you in the long run. I repeat: Properly investigating and legally protecting your idea *early* is the key to successful product development. The cost of discussing your idea for a few hours with a good attorney is more than outweighed by the benefits you will reap over time from having done so. And finally, remember: In this context as in any other, only a fool has himself/herself as his/her lawyer.

PATENTS

You may be wondering exactly what it is that you should, and can, patent. The answer is easily illustrated with something that we all have in our home: the toaster.

Let's say you have invented the very first toaster—a metal box containing a metallic wire that toasts your bread. With this invention, you have earned for yourself a *utility patent*. That's one type of patent.

But let's say instead that a toaster product already exists and is patented. You come up with the idea of adding plastic panels of some sort to the outside of the toaster so that people can touch the outside of the toaster without burning their hands. Your idea has added *functionality* to the toaster. Like the original toaster patent itself, your improved toaster would also qualify for a utility patent. The same principle would apply if you were the genius who decides to add the light/dark dial. Basically any useful *functioning feature* of an existing invention would qualify as a utility patent and is patentable in and of itself.

Similarly, if you take that toaster and add a new design element to it, say, rounded corners on the box itself, you can apply for a *design patent* for that decorative element. It is important to note, however, that if the toaster itself is still under its original patent (a patent lasts only for a limited time), simply adding rounded corners would not allow you to also sell the toaster. While you would own the patent on rounded corners, someone else would own the patent on the toaster itself. You could not sell any toaster without permission—as you would be infringing upon that person's patent—just as he or she could not sell any toaster with rounded corners without your permission. This is the stuff successful licensing deals are made of, and your patent attorney can help you understand and navigate these tricky legal waters.

The shorthand for this design patent versus utility patent difference is aesthetics versus function. It is important to understand, in terms of design, that design patents are intended to protect the ornamental and cosmetic aspects of products; they are *not* intended to protect their function. In an application for a design patent, the invention is described entirely in the drawing, not in the words accompanying it. For example, let's say you found that covering an existing metal toaster box with corners made of thick plastic looks the best, and so that's how you depicted your product in filing for the patent application. Assume now that you were granted the design patent for rounded corners on the toaster. Even if your new *design* also served the *function* of reducing the heat of the toaster box, you have a design patent—not a utility patent—so only the design, and not the function, is protected. Someone else could use plastic to reduce the toaster's heat and, as long as it didn't also feature rounded corners, there's nothing you could do about it (unless you took the action below).

For a utility patent, the amount of protection it provides is only as good as the description in words provided for the invention in its patent application. With the situation above, an additional filing for a utility patent would have solved the problem as described and given you protection over the heat-reducing function of the plastic corner as well. A good patent attorney is key, and he/she would have told you that, ultimately, you would have needed two patent applications for this: one for the design feature and the other for the functionality or utility.

One more consideration in the world of patents concerns those patents that have expired and are no longer effective. When a patent expires, it enters the *public domain.* This means that all inventors can use the patented item, adapting it as they see fit and in any way they want. For instance, anyone can make a television nowadays. The traditional components of a television have existed for years; their patents have long expired, and those inventions now belong to the public. Just as no one could stop you from using these inventions to manufacture a new brand of television, you couldn't stop anyone else either. However, if you improve the television, adding new components that affect functionality or design, you can patent that, and only you can use that *new* component. For example, the television, toward the beginning of its inception, had cathode-ray tubes. Those were later replaced by picture tubes. Eventually, someone learned how to take the images we see and make them color. And, later still, someone else invented the high-definition version of the television. Each item was a television, but each improvement was unique and patentable.

APPLYING FOR YOUR PATENT

Advice from the Pros

An inventor has only one year from the time of public disclosure to patent an invention. If the patent search comes back clear and the patent attorney advises that it is worth pursuing, an application should be filed as soon as possible.
—Jason M. Drangel, Esq., IP attorney, Epstein Drangel Bazerman & James LLP

Applying for patents can be expensive. You'll want to get the costs laid out well ahead of time and adjust your budget accordingly (see Figure 4–2). Overall, the process typically takes 18 to 24 months. (You do not have to sit idle during this time, however; as you will see from the rest of the book, there are many things you can be doing while you go through the patent process.) There are several Web sites, including About.com and USPTO.gov, that give you step-by-step details on these, but if you have questions, it's always best to consider consulting with an attorney—just to be certain there are no lingering legal questions to come back and bite you later.

IP Search: $700 to $1,000

Filing for patent, dependent on the subject matter:
  Utility Patents: A relatively simple application, $5,000 and $10,000 (including government fees, drawings, and other necessary disbursements.)

  Design Patents: May be charged on a fixed-fee basis, approximately $800 to $1,800

  Drawings (the U.S. Patent Office provides information for the specs needed for filing) per page: Approximately $125 to $150

  Government Fees: Approximately $215

Figure 4–2   Costs involved with filing for a patent.

One money-saving option is a *provisional patent.* Costing only several hundred dollars, the provisional patent lasts one year and gives you time to test, or test market, your item before filing for a full (nonprovisional) patent, which can end up costing several thousand dollars, as detailed in Figure 4–2.

Also, by filing for either a nonprovisional or provisional patent you preserve your rights on an international level. You have one year from the time of the U.S. application filing to file overseas. Having that right preserved can be perceived as a valuable asset and great selling point to potential investors or licensees. The preservation of these rights internationally is important, especially for countries of manufacturing like China, Taiwan, and then other great consumer markets such as the European markets. If you don't file a U.S. patent application or a provisional patent before you make public use of or offer the product for sale, you will lose those foreign rights.

Another consideration is that your product idea may change gradually over time. If you have already patented your item and an important element changes, you can always file for a "modification" to your patent or even file for a second patent altogether. Obviously there are additional fees connected to these options.

Also, consider the fact that patents do expire. And that is okay. While the patent exists, you will be provided two major benefits: (1) Your product will have a higher value (assuming your product is desirable to the market) because no competition can just jump in and undercut your price; and (2) in the case of something truly unique, your patent will allow you to be the "first to market." That is, you will be the first one to bring the product to the consumer market.

Advice from the Pros

Having a patent application filed will render your idea more valuable to possible investors or business partners by providing exclusivity in the marketplace. The more developed the intellectual property rights to your idea, the more valuable your idea will be.

—Peter D. Murray, Esq., IP attorney, Cooper & Dunham LLP

Being first to market often makes you the product leader in your particular category. People often respect and trust the company that created a particular product, whether it's Sharper Image's Ionic Breeze, or the Chia Pet, or Orange Glo (they were the first to market orange cleaner on a broad scale). The first to market establishes itself as "the" brand, so even if you do not have a patent (like Orange Glo), and other companies enter the market (like every other household products company that added oranges to their formulas), your product will be recognized as "the original," and it will generally sell the best. Sometimes being first to market is even more important than having a patent. Besides Orange Glo, just think of the many products that you see that are marked with the words "the original."

If after your research you determine your product does not infringe on others' (a must before going to market!) but, for one reason or another, it is still not patentable, it does not mean that you should not go forward. Because not having a patent is not a reason to stop. First to market can still win out.

Patents expire in 20 years or sooner from the filing date depending on certain factors (again, consult Web sites, the U.S. Patent Office, and/or an attorney). So not only do you want your product to be first to market, you also want it to be the only one out there for as long as possible.

Yes, patent issues can get overwhelming at times, in terms of both cost and general logistics. But instead of focusing on the difficulties, remember that the most important factor is to get your product to market. Don't let the patent process hold you back. Keep in mind that while a patent affords you certain protection, it does not stop someone or some company from finding a way to do something similar (maybe better, maybe worse, but similar nonetheless), and their idea may have come entirely from reading the patent application that *you* filed. (Think of that as a minor warning: You're not the only one doing research out there.) The bottom line: Patents can be circumvented, so your focus should always remain on getting your product to work the way you want, and once it is ready for the market, your focus should be on getting it out into the marketplace as soon as possible.

So do your due diligence and finish your research, work with your patent attorney (if you went that route), determine all the aspects of your product that will make it right for the marketplace, and then, as always, *keep moving . . .*

 ### Direct Response Marketing Success Story

"Ab Seat"—Protecting Your Idea

When I began to enter the prototype development stage of an ab exercise product I was working on, I knew in this particular case I would not be marketing the product myself.

(continued)

As this product was being developed for the purposes of being licensed to an infomercial marketing company, it was more important than ever that I made sure I was buttoned-up in terms of my legal protection.

Not only did I complete all the appropriate patent searches, I also made sure NDAs were presented to all I spoke with on this particular project. Specifically the factory I was working with on development.

Though I have a long-standing relationship with this factory, I still required that they acknowledge our working relationship in the form of an NDA, with some work-for-hire language added. This specified that all aspects, improvements or otherwise, belonged to me, and that they would not develop a similar functioning product.

It turned out to be a good thing that I did. I entered into a licensing agreement shortly after I completed development of my product. The first requirement I needed to fulfill for my marketing partner was a copy of the agreement with my factory to ensure that "they (the factory) can not and will not manufacture a similar item." In addition, the marketing company (my licensee) wanted to ensure that it was clear to the factory that they had no ownership rights in this product. Having fulfilled all that, the marketing company then conducted their own patent search and we were ready to move forward.

Bottom line: had I not put in place all of the appropriate paperwork, and thus a paper trail, even with a known, well-trusted entity, I would not have been able to secure my licensing deal as fast and as easy as I had and, not to mention, at very favorable terms.

KEY CONCEPTS TO REMEMBER

1. Always consult a lawyer who specializes in intellectual property.

2. Non-disclosure agreements (NDAs) allow you to share and speak freely about your idea while protecting your rights to that idea.

3. NDAs should be used whenever you are about to enter into a business relationship for your idea.

4. The first step with your attorney is to determine if you can protect your idea.

5. From the legal perspective, properly investigate your idea as early on as possible.

6. Your attorney will determine if you can potentially protect your idea and also ensure that it does not infringe on others' ideas.

7. Do not be deterred if you cannot patent your product because there are many ways you can still go to market.

8. There are two basic types of patents:
   (1) *Utility*:   Protects functionality.
   (2) *Design*:   Protects decorative element.

9. Utility patents are only as good as the description of the invention in words, thus a good patent attorney is key to the inventor's protection.

10. *Public domain* refers to information, patent or otherwise, that anyone in the public can use—for our purposes, that would refer to expired patents.

11. The patent application process can take 18 to 24 months and can be expensive.

12. Provisional patents are an inexpensive option that can preserve your rights for up to one year.

13. Patent rights, whether nonprovisional or provisional, can be perceived as a valuable asset to potential investors, marketing companies, and others.

5

Manufacturing

Now that you have your functioning, working prototype, you should familiarize yourself with the manufacturing process. It may turn out that you will not have to worry about the manufacturing side of the business, depending on which route you go with your product. In many cases, if you are looking, and willing, to sell off your idea—or license your product—a prototype is all you need. The company that is fortunate enough to license or purchase your product should be able to handle all of the aspects of manufacturing themselves; if they are not, then it is not a company you want to be working with.

You should seriously consider whether or not you want to handle the manufacturing aspect of your product on your own. The prospects of manufacturing could be daunting, not to mention expensive—possibly very expensive. Should you decide that this is the route you want to go, this chapter will provide you with some great resources to arm yourself with, and it will provide a foundation for your understanding of the process so you will have some idea of what to expect.

Keep in mind that manufacturing can get expensive because

gearing up for the production of a product requires many things, from engineering drawings to tooling and molds (the cost for these can run anywhere from a few thousand dollars up to and possibly above $50,000). There are some ways to offset some of the costs, and I will discuss them as well.

At this stage you should take a look at what you have and evaluate your goals and objectives. A good goal is to bring your product from concept to working prototype, to prove the validity of your idea. A good objective is to make money from your idea. The choices are simple: License or sell your idea to a manufacturer or distributor, or manufacture your own product and take it to market yourself. The direction to choose can be a little more complicated. The manufacturing route can prove very profitable, but please understand that there are financial requirements and risks involved. The choice of a license or sale of your idea is less expensive, and it does allow you to pursue other opportunities or invent more products (because once you license your product, the company you align with will take over, and, hopefully, you will just sit back and collect royalty checks (licensing your product is discussed in detail in Appendix A at the end of this book).

WORKING WITH A MANUFACTURER

In either case, you should understand the manufacturing process—what it entails, how to approach it, and how to get the most from it at various levels. So let's begin. From your prototype you will need to provide the manufacturer with hard-line drawings or engineering drawings. These are functional diagrams that give specifications for your product's particular manufacturing requirements. For example, if your product requires a motor, the drawings need to indicate the kind of motor, or if it requires gears, the drawings need to indicate the size of the gears and how they fit together. All of these specifications need to be illustrated: gear ratios, motor types, thicknesses, and types of materials used. And all measurements need to be carefully detailed for manufacturing purposes. These drawings, along with your prototype, will ensure the manufacturing or preproduction (prior to manufacturing) stage goes smoothly or at least without too many hurdles. The more details you provide to your manufacturer, the less you will have to modify your product once you begin manufacturing.

Sound overwhelming? Don't worry; in many cases the factory will be able to help you with this process. Since you should have a well-developed prototype at this point, they should be able to work with that and *reverse engineer* (the process of reversing how the item was put together and its functionality) what you have created. The factory may even offer suggestions for alternative materials or parts and offer suggestions in terms of functionality as it relates to manufacturing. Throughout your research for your prototype, you may have spoken to plastics manufacturers or electronics engineers and others who may have knowledge that can help you see your invention through to its final destination: people's homes. You may have found out that you needed a certain motor or a certain type of gear or that there was a concern regarding the type of plastic, metal, or other material that would work best with your product. All of these details will come out in the prototype stage. Continual change is part of the progression toward the perfect product as you begin to get into the manufacturing stage. Either way, the types of materials and the composition of the parts are very important. So during the development process, you do want to make sure you have consulted an expert in those areas to optimize the choices of the materials to be used to ensure functionality and control costs. If you used a professional prototype company, it will be able to direct you in that regard. In the event you did not have expert opinions in the building of the prototype, not to worry because that expertise can be obtained from the factory you choose to manufacture your product. The factory can suggest alternative materials and the like both for functionality purposes and ease of manufacturing. Just ask for their help, and they will be happy to accommodate.

Advice from the Pros

We always help with the design and engineering of a product. We have an engineering team to help with product development and another engineering team to adjust the product for the smoothest and most efficient production. We also offer advice on the best, most common, and most reasonably priced materials to use for your components.

—Victor Wai, factory owner, China

Direct Response Marketing Success Story

The Sun Visor: Asking the Experts

Years ago, I had developed a sun visor for cars. What I had envisioned was a specific product that utilized specialty glass, and I was familiar with what I wanted it to do and how it should function. Nevertheless, because of the nature of the material (glass) and the application of its use (the car), I knew I had to be concerned about safety first. So I started at the library (this was pre-Internet). I located some books on different types of glass and plastics used in cars and the properties of those materials. From shatter resistance to heat sensitivity to durability and so on; once I had a base of knowledge, I called experts. I started with Corning glass (known for their glass manufacturing and fiber optics equipment (which is formed from glass). I asked questions, and the company proved very helpful in sending samples and directing me accordingly.

Lesson: By not being fearful of sharing my idea with the kind people at Corning, the company became an invaluable resource for my product development—and we found the most effective material with the best price.

When I conceived the idea for my paper lunch bags with four-color printing on all sides, I already knew from a technology standpoint that it could be accomplished. However, I did not know if specifically what I needed could be achieved. In this case, I had already known that price was an issue for the consumer and that my ultimate product would be competing with plain brown (inexpensive) bags. As such, I knew I could not sell my product if each one of my bags had to sell for $1.00 or more.

I started with calls to local manufacturers and distributors in the New York area (I lived in New York City, and the best place to start is near your hometown) for paper bags and inquired about the details of placing an order. Now, at this point I was still in my trust-no-one stage, and I did not want to share my million-dollar idea with anyone, especially a company that I perceived as able to easily take my idea. And to ask them to sign an NDA would not make sense because the idea wasn't quite fully formed as yet—I was just exploring. I was very unspecific as to what exactly I needed, but I asked my question: "Can you custom print in four colors on a brown bag about the size of a lunch bag?" And so began my product realization stage and the steps toward manufacturing.

The first company said it could not do four-color printing; they were limited to two-color printing, but this company told me who *could* do it. So I called *them*. When I spoke to this next company, their representatives explained that, like the first company I had called, they could do only two-color printing as well. But they gave me another company to call, . . . and so on went this process of calling printers. In the meantime, with each conversation, I gained more and more knowledge about bag manufacturing and printing. I learned about the different types of printing and the different types of bags. And after all of my questions with all of these companies, because I was open to dialogue and was listening and learning, I became somewhat of an expert. I subsequently found one of the largest printed-bag manufacturers in the country, and that company was not only willing to help me launch my product, it was also excited to work with me to perfect the idea and the product and to achieve the best possible costs. See Chapter 1 for the results!

Get to know your product and its components. Never be afraid to ask questions of the experts. As your parents or teachers may have told you, "There are no stupid questions." They were right. Become knowledgeable about all the components needed to make *your* item a working, real-world product, and you will find it helps to further ground you in the world of successful DR marketing. You do not have to divulge secrets or tell people anything you don't want to tell them. Just tell them you're calling because you may be purchasing their services. It's okay to speak in generalities, but do sound professional and do sound as though you're genuinely interested in doing business with them—this is their life, and what you're asking about will become yours. And remember, people are always happy to share their expertise on a particular subject with someone else.

Remember your objective: What you're really looking for is the lowest-cost option that maintains the integrity and functionality of the product with the best possible materials. You want to create a quality product, but you're going to want to do it at the lowest cost possible. Sometimes this comes down to materials, other times it's the process by which your product is put together and/or the use of existing components that can be utilized in constructing your invention. Sure, your item can be made of platinum and work on a complex electrical system guided by infrared. But the guy (or gal) who builds the same item out of wood and aluminum and gives the consumer the same results at one-third the price, that's who wins. Obviously, being first to market and obtaining patent protection all play a part in this, but the point remains the same: If you have a product that is too costly and thus not accessible to the general public, all you will have is a great patent, not a successful consumer product. Maintain quality, do not sacrifice your product's integrity, but keep your consumer in mind.

Advice from the Pros

Product quality is important. Don't sell empty boxes. Only undertakers can sell empty boxes and get away with it.
—Ron Popeil

FINDING A MANUFACTURER

Now that you're armed with the knowledge, you need to find a manufacturer.

For domestic production ("Made in the U.S.A."), there are many resources, and the best place to start is the Internet. Pure plastic items, paper products, and even skin-care, hair-care or other solution-based products can be easily sourced in the United States and priced competitively. In the early stages, domestic factories may be the way to go because you can usually find factories willing to produce small quantities and leave you with a good amount of control over the initial stage of manufacturing. This initial stage is very important, as you want to ensure that the quality is what you want, and, in many cases, you will learn there are changes that have to be made. These changes can be due to a variety of issues, from functionality to manufacturing in mass production. You will most likely find that you have to alter components, design, and the like. But take your time, and get it right. It is more important that your product is right. Do not rush to get it to the market for financial reasons or for the seasonality of an item. When you rush, you lose. I am asked all the time by both inventors and company clients, "When is the best time to bring a product to market?" and my answer is always the same: "When it is ready!"

If you want the least expensive approach and are ready to do some work, China is the way to go. We see it every day on the news and read about it all the time in the newspapers: China is like no other place when it comes to manufacturing. The sheer size of their available workforce cannot be matched, and the government provides the factories with financial assistance in many cases. Thus, with their low labor costs and government subsidies, China is well positioned to provide the most for the least. But you have to stay on top of the entire process, and pay attention carefully not because they cannot be trusted—just the contrary!—but because it is still a foreign country and it is still far away. There are not only language barriers but also cultural differences that come into play. Don't be afraid to try this alternative for manufacturing; just be aware that you will need to pay attention to it. Take your time, communicate carefully, and again, be open to learning, but forge ahead and *keep moving* . . .

Advice from the Pros

Almost everyone in the United States or Europe is trying to get products made for the lowest cost he or she can arrange. China should be the first thought in their mind. I have a quality-control team traveling to factories all over China to inspect the merchandise that is supplied to my customers. The most important thing is that we provide inspection services before the goods ship to the client, to ensure that they receive the proper item in good condition.

—Victor Wai, factory owner, China

The Hong Kong Trade Council is a fantastic, and expansive, source for finding manufacturers in China [go to www.tdctrade.com/ (see Figure 5–1)]. They have a tremendous database of suppliers for electronics, gifts, and housewares, and every other category you can think of. They provide listings of the factories with names of contacts. They also list *trading companies*, which are companies that represent many factories across several product categories. Trading companies can be an enormous help, as they work not only with one factory but several in a particular product category, and thus they can help you achieve the best possible pricing. They can also help with the manufacturing of low-cost prototypes in the early stages.

Note that there are also local, U.S.–based sourcing and trading companies that can help you work with manufacturers in China. These U.S.–based trading companies are great to work with too. There is usually an American person with a wealth of experience of manufacturing in China who therefore has a counterpart in China. This helps resolve most "lost-in-translation" issues that occur. Many of

What are you looking for? Help us serve you better!

tdctrade.com 香港貿易發展局 Hong Kong Trade Development Council

| Home | Sourcing | Hong Kong Trade Events | Worldwide Trade Events | Market Intelligence | Industry Focus | Small Business Resources |

Precision sourcing from tdctrade.com

繁體中文 · 简体中文

Your Language

日本語 · Deutsch · Español
Français · Italiano · Português
한국어 · العربية · Русский

TDC Integrated Marketplace

Sourcing

Top Searched Products:

* Gemset Jewellery
* Semi-precious Stone Jewellery
* Tee & Sweat Shirts
* Plastic Photo Frame
* Leather & Suede Handbag
* Jewellery Watch
* Web Camera
* Digital Camera
* Magnetic / Smart Card Reader
* Diamond Jewellery
* Electronic Diet Scale

more ▶

Find Products

Go

Exhibitions

* Hong Kong International Jewellery Show 2007 (6-10 Mar)
* FILMART 2007 (20-23 Mar)
* Hong Kong Electronics Fair 2007 (Spring Edition) (14-17 Apr)

more ▶

Product Magazines

View Electronic Version:

more ▶

Search

All ▼ Go >>

Advanced Search | Help

Hot Keywords :
iPod, REACH, RoHS, textile, green manufacturing, EuP, CEPA, QDII

About HKTDC

Need help?

φ Contact Us
Our global network

* HKTDC Services
* HKTDC News & Speeches

About tdctrade.com
Partners & Affiliates
Awards & Honours
Site Map

e-Newsletters
* tdctrade.com express
* SME News Flash
* HK Trader

Features

High commercial potential for biotechnology industry in HK
Biotechnology industry is an emerging business in Hong Kong with high commercial potential. Hong Kong is well known for its research capabilities, especially in discovering and testing new infectious diseases such as SARS and bird flu ...▶

Diamond cutter takes a shine to China
A leading Belgian diamond cutter is amazed that he was able to achieve an extraordinarily high level of success in Asia in just two years ▶..

STYLE HONG KONG **HONG KONG Brands to Enter China Market**

Fast Paths

▶ Sourcing ▶ Hong Kong Trade Events ▶ Worldwide Trade Events

Buy and sell quality products from Hong Kong, the Chinese mainland and Taiwan.

* Buy / Sell Products
* Bids n Offers
* TDCLink
* Product Magazines

Enter email address

SUBSCRIBE NOW! FREE !

Modify SUBSCRIPTION

View Past Issues

Figure 5–1 Hong Kong Trade Council home page.

(Figure continued on next page)

* Hong Kong Directory

Exhibitions and conferences by HKTDC and other organisations.
* HKTDC Exhibitions
* SME Events
* Other Exhibitions & Conferences

Trade events around the world.
* Service Industry Events
* Manufacturing Industry Events
* Hong Kong-organised Events

▶ Market Intelligence

Latest market news and analysis by country/region.
* Hong Kong Economy
* China Trade
* International Markets
* Emerging Markets
* Webcast
* Bookshop (New Titles)
* Business-Stat Online
* Business Guide:China, US, EU
* Business Alert:China, US, EU
* Hong Kong Trade Quarterly

▶ Industry Focus

Latest news, trends and business leads by industry.
* Design, Innovation & Licensing
* Electronics & Electricals
* Garments & Textiles
* Gifts & Houseware
* Technology
* Toys & Sporting Goods
* Timepieces & Jewellery
* Transport & Logistics
* More

▶ Small Business Resources

One-stop source of trade events and online tools for small businesses.
* Resources Centre
* Free Advisory Service
* SME Forum
* Premier Connect
* Business Tools
* Business InfoCentre
* Travel Visa Application
* Photo Library

in video or audio format

Add tdctrade.com RSS Feeds RSS

Figure 5–1　(*Continued*)

these trading companies, or import companies, have been providing their services for a long time, and they have excellent access to manufacturing resources. Furthermore, they have dealt with so many different types of products that they probably have seen something similar to yours and can really help. The downside of working with a U.S.–based trading company is that it will cost you more to purchase your final product than it would cost if you used a foreign importer. However, the time you will save, the efficiency of the importer's service, and its expertise will more than pay for themselves. And actually at this stage if you did venture off on your own to source overseas, you would probably end up paying more for your product because you are not familiar with what you should be paying. In that case, the U.S.–based import company can be worth its weight in gold.

Whichever way you go, do your due diligence by speaking with various companies. When communicating with the companies directly in China, you will find e-mail works well. The manufacturers in China are always are able to communicate in English, although they are often not completely fluent. Overall, however, you should have no problem conversing with them.

When communicating, keep your message short and simple. Speak (or write) using bulleted points, listing your objectives and questions. This will allow them to focus on one item at a time. They will answer everything, and they will be thorough. Remember, if you succeed, they succeed—you get business, they get business. Everyone makes money, and everyone wins.

When you are ready to start the process you can send them an NDA so that you can feel assured you have the same kinds of protections you'd have if you were speaking to a domestic designer or prototype company.

Advice from the Pros

Most of our inventors believe in signing nondisclosure agreements. So do we.
—Victor Wai, factory owner, China

There is even a section within the Web site referred to above where you can get bids from potential manufacturers that will help you save on your final product cost. But at this point you do not want to put your product out to more than a few factories because you're simply trying to determine the average costs of having your product made.

Many people still want to manufacture within the United States, but the fact remains that volume-based mass production is more cost efficient overseas, for all of the reasons we discussed above. Again, if it's the United States you want and you are starting with small quantities, then working with a domestic source does have its advantages. It provides you with the ability to see your product being produced without traveling halfway around the world. And there is no greater pleasure than seeing that first one roll off the production line. Having an ongoing dialogue with the people producing your product goes a long way too, and if you are there watching, you can be immediately available to work through any kinks that may arise. In other words, if your manufacturing is easily accessible, then you can maintain more control. But going overseas can cut your costs in half or even more, and a good trade agent will be able to help you through any rough patches.

My printed lunch bags were all manufactured domestically. I spent a great amount of time at the factory, and, because of my visits, the owners not only helped me perfect my product but I was also able to help them push their methods and improve on their processes, which they were able to apply to the needs of other customers. Thus, whether you choose a factory close to home or venture off overseas, do plan to spend time at the factory, especially for your first production run.

If you have any uncertainties regarding the company with which you are about to do business, take advantage of the Internet. Do your research, speak with people, and trust your instincts. If someone asks something of you that does not make sense at first, don't do it. Wait until you are sure it is the right way, or you are least comfortable from an intellectual standpoint on your own. You are smart enough to have invented your item, so you are smart enough to understand what makes sense and what does not. And don't underestimate the usefulness and value of U.S.–based importers and trade agents. But whatever you do, whichever path you take, do not let the obstacles stop you. They are a reason to pause for a moment and take some time to think ahead, but do not stop. Continue on, keep pushing, and *keep moving . . .*

Advice from the Pros

The three most important things the inventor should look for in the factory he or she selects are (1) the history of the factory, (2) the abilities of the engineering team, and (3) the management of the factory. The inventor should look for a factory or an agent who is progressive and shows honest leadership, good management, and adequate financing.

—Victor Wai, factory owner, China

Direct Response Marketing Success Story

Price Point and the Marketplace versus Price Point and the Factory

I worked with a company that was manufacturing a product with a retail selling price of $49.99: a multipiece tool kit. It was a terrific item, and it had many uses, but the sales were weaker than the client expected.

So what did the client do?

The client considered different marketing options and other promotional programs. Ultimately, they decided to make one very aggressive change: They lowered their price to $39.99. They realized an immediate increase in sales of more than 30 percent. But now they had a profit margin concern because a seller cannot cut a price without its affecting how much he or she will profit.

Now their manufacturing challenge began.

They already had a well-established factory manufacturing the product for them in Taiwan where the quality is high, but so is the cost of labor and operations relative to China. The client did not want to sacrifice quality or product integrity, and they wanted to be careful not to pressure their existing factory and thus hurt their relationship.

When they came to me with the issue, I began the process by approaching it very carefully, starting on the outside. First, I spoke

(continued)

with several China-based factories, identifying the factories that produced precision items already within the category. I provided the existing production samples and requested from the new potential factories *countersamples*—that is, sample products of similar form and function that were being produced by their facility. Generally, countersamples are actually factory-made duplicates of the items presented, but at this point in this situation, we just wanted to gauge the factory's current ability.

With countersamples in hand and price quotes close to 50 percent less than what the current cost was, we now had enough knowledge on the manufacturing marketplace to approach their current factory. The objective was to show respect *for* them while we earned respect *from* them. This was accomplished by acknowledging their help in launching the program while also showing them how well versed we had become in the actual manufacturing process and cost of the product.

We finally had a meeting with the factory during which we discussed two main points: First, we brought up the sales increase which had occurred because of the reduction in retail price. Second, we mentioned our ability to source the manufacturing of a similar-quality product at a lesser price elsewhere. With the former information, the factory immediately recognized that there would be an increase in manufacturing efficiencies and a faster return on investment (ROI) for manufacturing set-up costs. With that, coupled with the subtle hint of our obtaining alternate sourcing elsewhere, they offered a solution. The factory lowered the cost of production to help with margins at the new retail price point of $39.99, and they suggested instead of our sacrificing any quality and starting with a new factory, that *they* would offer us a two-tier program, whereby they would provide a slightly lesser quality unit (still greatly functional but changed sufficiently to enable them to produce more pieces per day) and adjust the number of units in the kit to reflect a smaller piece count, allowing for a new product altogether at a new retail price of just $19.99, for the more price sensitive market. This gave them a two-tier marketing program and an opportunity to appeal to a broader demographic across several markets.

Lesson: Always remember that there is a direct correlation between the price of your item and the size of your potential customer base. The best approach with any factory is to take your time in gathering your facts.

KEY CONCEPTS TO REMEMBER

1. Offshore factories and suppliers such as those in China can be an invaluable resource, but for many reasons, they can also be somewhat difficult to control and manage. So consider all aspects of manufacturing your product before deciding if you will manufacture it in the United States or elsewhere.

2. The factory can serve not only as a pure manufacturer of your product, but also as an advisor to you during the final development phase of your project. The factory can, for example, suggest the best materials to use or the best approaches to ultimately build a better product.

3. When determining price based on chosen materials and product configuration, realize that the higher the retail selling price, the smaller your customer base. The lower your retail price point, the more accessible your product, and thus the larger your potential customer base.

4. As a side note to price point: Look at your category. If most products in that category sell for under $30, you may have to reconsider your product's functionality or materials if you have a planned retail selling price of $100.

5. Your managing the manufacturing of your product can be overwhelming to you as well as very expensive.

6. Although having a basic understanding of the manufacturing aspects is important and helpful, for your first project you should strongly consider licensing your product to an existing and experienced company.

THE INFOMERICAL AND OTHER DIRECT RESPONSE MARKETING TECHNIQUES

6

Assessing Your Product for the Infomercial and/or Direct Response Market

---

(Or, Is Your Product Right for DR?)

If your heart's picked up the pace a bit, that's understandable. You've come a long way, and the next step will really throw you into the modern inventor's world.

It's now time to understand the fundamentals of direct response marketing. And just so we're all on the same page (figuratively and literally I guess): DR deals with products that go direct to the consumer via the television infomercial, radio, or print and direct mail, avoiding retailers ("brick-and-mortar" stores).

While this chapter will help you assess your product for DR marketing, the following chapters (7 and 8) will break down the infomercial for you, detailing pros and cons as well and what to expect as you approach this phase of your creation. We'll also touch on alternative marketing approaches such as the Web, shopping channels, and even the "grassroots" approach to launching and marketing your product.

Direct response marketing also includes direct mail, which can be anything from the strip connected to your credit card bill asking you to order a product to a small slip of paper inside a coupon book advertising your creation, as well as print and radio advertising geared directly to the consumer. However, this book is about DR TV, and while the chapters to follow fork into the Web and home shopping networks, we will still end up back at DR TV.

The first thing to do is discern whether or not your product is right for DR marketing. As we began in Chapter 2 looking at the basics, we are now going to continue to complete our determination and understanding of whether or not your product is right for DR marketing.

The Fundamentals of a DR TV Product

1. *Mass appeal:*   Everyone will need one.
2. *Highly demonstrable:*   Its uses can be easily shown.
3. *High perceived value:*   Looks expensive, does six jobs in one, or is a time-saver.

An inventor once came to me with a great idea: Decorative computer mouse covers. Now, millions of houses have computers, and people love to make their computers pretty. But, although it's a great idea, mouse covers do not fit several of the necessary criteria for DR. First, they don't solve a problem. Next, they're not demonstrable in their functionality—as attractive as they may be, there's just nothing compelling to show TV viewers. And while many households *can* use it, there is little *need* for a decorative item, and it does not solve a problem, which diminishes the *perceived value*. So let's look at the checklist on page 81 called "The Six Questions of a DR Product."

The reason the six questions in the box are important is that they speak to the fundamentals of DR marketing. While not all of those questions need a "yes" answer for your item to be successful, the more yeses you have, the better your chances are. (Keep in mind that there is no "sure thing," but starting off at the strongest possible position will vastly improve your chances to succeed.)

The Six Questions of a DR Product

Yes   *No*

☐   ☐   1. Does it solve a problem?

☐   ☐   2. Is it easy to use?

☐   ☐   3. Is it something every *household* can use (does it have mass appeal)?

☐   ☐   4. Can it be clearly and easily demonstrated? (The "demo" or "Wow" factor)

☐   ☐   5. Will it have a high "perceived value," yet be affordable (priced right)?

☐   ☐   6. Does your product appeal visually? (Does it have curb appeal?)

So let's begin the process with the question, "Does your product solve a problem?" This is a very important one, and the answer to it forms the basis for beginning your DR evaluation. If your product solves a problem, perhaps by making something faster to accomplish, cleaner than before, easier to do, or saves the consumer "much-needed counter space," it fills a *need*. And if your product does fill a need by solving a problem people encounter every day or it is something consumers are interested in, your product might very well be perceived as a must-have or one they "must order now," and that puts you ahead of the game.

Advice from the Pros

Ask yourself, "Does it simplify the manner in which a task is performed, and does it resolve, solve, or improve something that consumers would be concerned about and interested in?"
—Mike Sobo, president, SAS Group, a DR marketing company

Moving to the question "Is it easy to use?" and following your determining if your product solves a problem, it still needs to be easy to use and easy to explain. If your product needs to have two people turn a key simultaneously while someone else twists a crank and your neighbor readjusts a satellite antenna, perhaps this is *not* the product for DR marketing. Ice cream scoops, for instance—the old-fashioned ones with the thumb press—those are easy to use; not necessarily right for DR marketing, but certainly easy to use. The Ab Roller, the Chef Wizard, the Handy Stitch, and the Pasta Pro are all items that are easy to use, and were great for DR marketing, as all six questions can be answered with a "yes."

Now, hopefully, it does solve a problem, and it's easy to use, but "Is it something every household can use?" or "does it have mass appeal?" If you've developed a great item for the kids to use in the pool, this item, no matter how wonderful, has *limited appeal*. First, you need a household with children. Second, you need a household with a pool. While there are plenty of households across the United States with both a pool and kids who play in it, there are, for instance, many more households that have a car, a television, pictures to hang, walls to paint, and so on. Also, with the pool example, you're also dealing with a seasonality issue in most parts of the United States, and this too can hinder sales.

Of course, smaller categories are not a bad thing, they're just narrower. "Small categories," or niche markets, can be markets for products like something for your barbecue grill or a golf game, something that makes the bouquet of your favorite wine last longer, or, as above, a swimming item. Another way to think of it is "the better snow boot versus the better sneaker"—there are many people in the Northeast and Midwest who would love a snow boot that is comfortable, warm, and waterproof and that protects them from slipping on icy paths or walkways. But there are many more people that wear sneakers. This example shows one product that is good for everyone (the sneaker) and one that is a smaller-category, or niche-oriented, product. Again, there's a good chance you'll find success with the snow boot, and, although a good-sized market exists, DR is still a numbers game, so your likelihood of success through that venue is greatly reduced. The more people there are who can find interest or need in your product, the more likelihood there is for success.

One last note on niche markets: Sometimes a product that seems right for everyone is being sold at a retail selling price so high that it has greatly reduced its potential customer base. Well, that base could be broadened simply by altering the way in which the price is paid. The fitness category, for instance, covers young, old, male, and female. But your product may be not $19.99 or even $99.99 but $999.99—too expensive for most households. But by offering a payment plan, with a low initial payment, you easily expand the accessibility for your product. You are essentially allowing *all* households to get in on your product. A great example is the BowFlex. It sells for over $1,000, but the company offers a payment plan by which the customer can buy it with as little as a $19.99 initial payment. Then, of course, the customer pays off the balance over many months. By doing that, the company has made the product accessible to everyone from the college student to the well-heeled executive. And "it's less expensive per month than most gym memberships."

The bottom line here is the broader your audience, the larger the market and the higher the likelihood of success. From a DR perspective, by having the largest target audience possible for your product, you automatically provide more selling opportunity because you can advertise your product in more venues. In other words, if your product is solely for, say, science buffs, then you may be forced to limit your advertising to genre shows (for example, *Star Trek* reruns) or the TechTV channel. But if you've created a cooking item, well, everyone cooks—whether they're fans of *Star Trek* or not. The more people you reach, the more product you sell.

Because television is a visual medium, do not underestimate the value and importance of number 4 on our list: "Can it be clearly and easily demonstrated?" You have to have something to show your audience—you need a demo and you *need* the "Wow" factor.

People in general are impatient, and they need immediate satisfaction. So something visual needs to come across in the demonstrating of the product. But, more than that, if you can capture your audience —"with just a press of a button" or a "click of a switch" or even "a simple turn of a knob"—voilà, *something* happens that catches their eye, you're halfway there. Getting people to stop and look *is* half the battle.

As your demo is crucial in selling your product, evaluate your product carefully, determine if it can easily be demonstrated, and find its "wow" factor. You have to convey to consumers that your product is great and if you don't "catch" them, you may never have a chance to get that message across. So think of the best attention-grabbing way to demonstrate your product in action. If your product can be clearly and easily demonstrated, then you are one step closer to DR TV success. Later on in the process, your infomercial producer will help you further identify many more demos to help drive sales and achieve great success.

The high "perceived value" and visual appeal points (questions 5 and 6) are last but not least. They can be what makes the difference between success and failure—the difference between consumers' just nodding in approval and their picking up the phone and ordering. Will it be an offer they can't resist? Will the price, as compared to the value they see, be so great that they just can't believe it? "Can I solve that problem so easily with that or those, for just that much money?"

The perceived value and visual appeal go hand in hand and directly to what your viewer thinks your product is worth ("How much would *you* pay?"). If you've created a new kind of pot for use in the kitchen, no matter how good it is, the perceived value is relatively limited. So for $19.99 it may be great, but if your product is going to cost $119.99, you may quickly lose your audience because the need to solve the problem just isn't perceived as worth it. So it is not just how expensive it is perceived as visually but it is also how it is priced within its product category and related to the problem it solves.

Another aspect on the perceived-value characteristic is how big the offer is: How much are you giving away? For this, think: The 12-piece cooking set, the 30-piece kitchen set, the 100-piece sewing set, and so on. Perceived value relates not only to your specific product but also to your entire offer (consider the phrase "absolutely free" for more clarity). So think carefully about your product, and consider the way it looks AND everything you can include with it as part of your offer, and ask yourself again, "How much would I pay?"

Now that you have finished the questions and have a firm understanding of the elements and essence of those questions, it is possible that you do not have a "yes" to one or several of them. If that is the case and your answers are "no" to two or more of the above categories, it is more than likely that your product is not right for DR TV marketing , but it does not mean that your product will not be successful. You can look to several other means of marketing your product. You can try to sell direct to small retailers or direct to catalog companies. In looking to go this route, you should focus on small retailers near where you live or specialty catalog companies. Both are more open to taking in new products, and if you find one that focuses on products within your item's category, it could turn out to be a great proving ground for the marketability of your product—and help open doors in the future for more broader distribution. We go into this a little deeper further on in the book.

With your assessment of your product complete, you will need to look further into the infomercial and its different forms. Then you need to consider the alternatives or additional venues for marketing your product. The next two chapters do just that, so let's *keep moving . . .*

Direct Response Marketing Success Story

For a Bass, It Was a Surprising Fluke

The Big Mouth Billy Bass was a success that didn't seem like it should be. Its one main weakness was that it didn't fill a need or solve a problem. It was a novelty. And novelty items don't usually catch on in DR. But this product had started in retail where it had gained a cult following.

(continued)

Its proven success at specialty retail accounts caught the attention of DR companies. The unique novelty of this item—it was original, funny, satirized both a familiar sport and the familiar idea of having a fish on your wall, and was good for all ages—and its wide appeal, created a surprise DR hit.

Because of its success, it—pardon—spawned much in the way of competition, including the award winning Boogie Bass. I helped with the music licensing on this item, and it went on to be a No. 1 DR TV hit in 2000, selling millions of units.

Keep in mind, however, that although it did not solve a problem, it was easy to use, it had mass appeal, it was highly demonstrable, it was priced right, and it certainly appealed visually. Thus it covered five of "The Six Questions of a DR Product."

(An unrelated postscript: This was the item that brought me into the world of direct response marketing.)

Lessons:

1. You can never predict a product's success.

2. Be prepared for competition.

KEY CONCEPTS TO REMEMBER

1. Determine if your product is right for DR by ensuring that it covers the fundamentals:

   (1) Mass appeal

   (2) Highly demonstrable

   (3) High perceived value

2. Ask yourself the "Six Questions of a DR Product." The more questions you answer "yes" to, the higher the likelihood of success:

   (1) Does it solve a problem?

   (2) Is it easy to use?

   (3) Does it have mass appeal?

   (4) Can it be clearly and easily demonstrated?

   (5) Does it have a high perceived value?

   (6) Does it appeal visually?

3. Though there are steadfast rules by which products will have a chance for success, remember that there are no guarantees in the DR TV business.

7

The Infomercial

With our "Six Questions of a DR Product" answered in Chapter 6, you know whether or not you have the right elements to go forward with marketing a product through DR, so you are now ready to go to the next step: the making of the infomercial. Getting to the infomercial can be a long road, so I don't want to create any illusions that it's easy.

Advice from the Pros

Our advice to new marketers and inventors is to meet with respected DR TV experts, ask questions, and then *listen, listen, listen.* DR TV is not just about selling a product—it's about launching and building a successful ongoing business.

—Marcia Waldorf, partner and producer, Waldorf Crawford LLC

To shoot a commercial, you'll need a production company that knows how to create an infomercial (which will require a script, actors, a set, and so on), a media buying company to buy the space on the networks (local and regional cable most likely), a telemarketing group to take calls from consumers, and an order fulfillment center to actually fill those orders and send them out.

DR TV productions can be found in two style formats: short forms and long forms. Another way to put that is that an infomercial can be a 2-minute spot or a 28½-minute show.

SHORT-FORM INFOMERCIALS

Also called spots or two-minute spots, short-form infomercials generally have the following characteristics:

- *Length.* Two minutes. The time can be broken down further into 60-second and 30-second spots.
- *Product price range.* $14.99 to $39.99.
- *Purpose.* These are great ways to introduce new products to the marketplace in a relatively cost effective manner, as compared to traditional forms of advertising.
- *Structure.* These quickly provide information, show the product, demonstrate the product, provide great testimonials, make great offers, quote prices, give phone numbers, and take orders.

Pros

1. These are relatively inexpensive to produce and to purchase the media for.
2. They can be viewed seven days a week, at various times during the day.
3. They offer higher visibility than long-form infomercials because of the broader availability of ad space.

4. They provide a quick approach to the market because they can be produced quickly and cost effectively. Thus these productions enable you to get to market quickly and expand rapidly in the event of a success.

5. A short-form infomercial can be positioned easily throughout local, regional, and national cable channels, as well as network and syndicated TV channels, giving you the opportunity for widespread exposure for your product or just the same provide the ability to target specific demographic groups (for example, men only, women only, or sports enthusiasts).

6. They generate direct product sales, creating brand and product awareness for purposes of establishing retail distribution through mass marketers, catalogs, and other venues.

Cons

1. The short forms may not allow enough time to really draw in the viewers, to "hook them."

2. The short form is not a good venue for higher-priced products (very few priced above $19.99 do well).

3. The broadcasting time slots for short-form infomercials have become highly competitive due to larger companies' entering the fray (for example, Sears, Home Depot, and Sharper Image), making it harder to get noticed, and pushing advertising costs upward.

The Three Types of Short-Form Infomercials from an Advertising Perspective

1. *The sale.* The pure purpose is to sell your product.

2. *The lead generator.* A number is provided that asks you to "call for more information." Generally, this method is used

to sell higher-priced items that require more of sales pitch than two minutes allows.

3. ***The brand builder.***   This type showcases a product and is generally chosen for introducing a new product within a line, a new technology, or otherwise for purpose of highlighting a brand (building brand awareness). (Sears, Home Depot, Sharper Image, and Bowflex use these.)

The one you choose is dependent on the type of product or service being offered. For our purposes we will focus on the first type because you're developing and selling a new consumer product, not an established brand or a new service.

For short-form spots, you can purchase ad space for a fraction of the cost of typical traditional advertising—we will get into this more in the later chapter covering media buying. The spot is also a tried-and-true way to determine if customers will purchase your item. No matter how great your friends and family may tell you your product is, it is not until some objective viewer reaches for the phone, makes the call, and orders your item that you will really know if there is a demand for your product.

Advice from the Pros

Only in rare instances have products priced above $20 been successful in short form, the exceptions being products that were previously long-form products that were later reintroduced using short form to remind customers of the more detailed long-form presentation.

—Mike Sobo, president, SAS Group, DR marketing company

LONG-FORM INFOMERCIALS

The long-form infomercials are generally what people think of when they hear the term *infomercial*. The long forms usually have the following characteristics:

- *Length.* Usually 28½ minutes long.
- *Product price range.* $59.95 to $999.95. Higher-ticket items require more time to sell and explain so that the potential customer can understand and appreciate the value of the product.
- *Structure*
  - ° Three 6- to 7-minute segments about your product.
  - ° Three 2- to 3-minute segments presenting the offer, price, and phone number or the *call to action* (CTA). The offer is presented, and the viewer is invited to take action: "Call now . . . *Operators are standing by . . .* "
- *Purpose.* Long forms are great for introducing a new technology that is priced higher than would be a short-form item. It allows for a complete explanation and time with the customer. Also, it allows time to build product value and create a sense of urgency for the viewer to make the purchase, time to create an emotional connection, and time to show real-world benefits and emphasize the product's uniqueness.

Pros

1. Long forms generate direct product sales, creating brand and product awareness for purposes of establishing retail distribution through mass marketers, catalogs, and other venues.
2. Long forms provide great opportunities for product demonstrations and testimonials.

3. Long forms provide ample time to reinforce the product's value.

4. Long forms provide time to build emotional connections between products and viewers.

Advice from the Pros

Branding is often overlooked and should be considered in every phase from Web site to international marketing.
—Tara Borakos, president, Tara Productions, Inc.

Cons

1. Media time is usually late at night, though some great weekend day parts are available.

2. The cost can be prohibitive both because of the cost of production (the cost to produce infomercial itself) and the high cost of media. To gain visibility and product recognition, you have to run a show often. Over a long term, buying enough media time to gain a following and recognition can get very expensive, but doing so is a necessity to gain trust and sales.

When it comes to pricing for a short form, the rule of thumb does not *always* apply. Bowflex for instance, which is a $1,000-plus product, has been using the short-form spot as a way to increase visibility. This format also serves as a great form of brand building and brand awareness advertising in that it keeps the product out in front of the consumer, while supporting the continued run of the long-form shows. As the competitive landscape increases due to the entry of similar items, the marketing company has made a conscious effort to keep its brand in the forefront of everyone's mind when it comes to "getting in shape" through its short-form campaign.

OTHER INFOMERCIAL ISSUES TO KEEP IN MIND

Overall, infomercial marketing can be highly lucrative—that is why we're here. But the costs should be clearly understood, as well as the advantages and disadvantages of going this route altogether, whether in short form or long form. I have listed below some basic guidelines to keep in mind (more pros and cons).

Pros

1. DR TV is the fastest and best way to introduce a product to the consumer market and to ascertain if there's a true need or desire for it.

2. You'll get your product in front of the largest amount of people in the quickest amount of time.

3. It's the fastest approach of launching a product for a market whether it's regional or national.

4. You can easily gather informational sales data about your strategy and positioning of your product, to help confirm pricing and overall marketing approach.

5. You can build great professional alliances. Though you determine the destiny of your product, you work with profes-

sional producers, media buyers, and telemarketing companies who are there to help you in the process, and all of them will prove to be great partners for the duration of your program.

Cons

1. It's an all-or-nothing business to which you have to commit fully—both time and money.

2. It could be cost prohibitive. Not only is there the cost of producing the commercial but also the cost of buying the media and the necessary legal support to ensure that your claims and statements on TV for your product are legally accurate. There are also legal concerns on the product side (as previously discussed) just to get the product to this point.

3. Your product is immediately seen by many, which may increase your competition. If your product proves viable, it will quickly become known, and several other companies will jump into the category, possibly even before you have built a following for yours.

4. You may put a lot of time and money into designing your product, having a commercial produced, and having the product manufactured only to discover it's a flash-in-the-pan success (you manufacture a large amount of product based upon high initial demand that falls off quickly, leaving you with many extra units of your product) or, worse, a total bomb (you have spent as previously discussed only to discover there is no demand for your product) —part of the all-or-nothing aspect. But as a seasoned inventor, you can learn from your lack of success and go back to the drawing board, invent that next great product, and start again.

> ## Advice from the Pros
>
> If it can be sold for $19.95 or less, then short form is the way to go. If it is a high-ticket item or there is a story to tell, then long form is appropriate.
> —Tara Borakos, president, Tara Productions, Inc.

Those are some general rules and guidelines, as well as some of the most important details about the two forms of infomercials. This stage needs to be carefully entered into. It is expensive, it can be overwhelming, and it requires a lot in terms of not just money but understanding of the entire process.

A THIRD OPTION: LICENSING YOUR PRODUCT

Your first product is best licensed to a company within this business. Choose one that has a well-known name or has handled products that you are familiar with.

> ## Advice from the Pros
>
> The ERA is one of the few truly safe havens for inventors, providing an opportunity for shared ideas, feedback, and no ulterior motive. For example, check out the "New Product Hot Spot" at the ERA Web site (www.retailing.org).
> —Barbara Tulipane, president and CEO, Electronic Retailing Association

These companies have legal support, the financial wherewithal, the retail connections, and a full understanding of how to launch and roll out a product. There is not a seasoned professional in the business who will recommend that you raise the money and go at this alone. Take your time with the first one; a licensing deal can be very lucrative to you as well. And it can provide the financial windfall necessary to do the next one on your own.

Advice from the Pros

Find a company you trust and like working with. There are too many things that can go wrong, and the infrastructure you'd need to set up to run your project smoothly all on your own is costly and difficult to establish for one product.
—Denise DuBarry Hay, cofounder, Thane International, Inc.

However, there is a lot of support in this business, and people are willing to help. Should you not heed the advice of the pros on your first one, or should this not be your first foray into introducing product into the marketplace, and you have either raised the money or have the personal wherewithal financially, then go get 'em! But remember what I have said and understand the rules.

Of course, as with all things, people are bound to break the rules. Going it alone on your first product is not always a bad thing. There are a few examples of this; one that comes to mind is that of "Blue Stuff." This pain reliever product was founded by a gentleman near retirement age who first proved his item through local word-of-mouth advertising and then, after a successful few years, jumped into the world of infomercials, creating a number 1 infomercial and one of the most successful products in the business.

Again, look at the guidelines, and understand the formats. While the short form throws your product out there to the buyer quickly and efficiently and it gives your product high visibility, the long-form commercial will provide adequate time to tell the product's story, demonstrate the features and benefits, and allow you time to create the emotional connection for your viewer. Each is very different, and in the end, if you have determined your product is right for the infomercial venue, your price point will dictate which route you go.

Advice from the Pros

The process is both expensive and detailed and far more difficult than it appears on the surface.
—Mike Sobo, president, SAS Group, DR marketing company

But with either form, the goal is always the same: capture the viewers' attention and lead them to action (action = making a phone call) and make the sale.

JUST WHAT ARE THE COSTS?

One of the big cons that may have stood out to you in this chapter is that the infomercial can be cost prohibitive. The *minimum* investment in an infomercial from a reputable production company is $30,000 for a short form and $150,000 for a long form, and that is just the production cost. It does not include any product-related costs, celebrity spokespeople, or legal, initial media costs, or any other costs related to setting up for taking orders. All the initial costs amount to roughly anywhere from $75,000 to $300,000, respectively, through completion of initial media testing. If this road is not financially feasible, I strongly stress that you take a close look at the alternatives, some of which can *also* be utilized as components to DR TV marketing.

The alternatives, which also can be great additional venues for sales through the infomercial route, range from shopping channels to the Web. In addition, there are other approaches into the market that I discuss in the next chapter, such as a direct-to-retail approach through catalog, or even a grassroots approach, which basically builds a following via word of mouth and friends and family.

Advice from the Pros

Just like building a house, be prepared to have everything take longer and cost more than you expect. Have patience and do things the right way even if they take a little longer.
—Denise DuBarry Hay, cofounder, Thane International, Inc.

Direct Response Marketing Success Story

The Magic Vest: Lose Weight Fast, But How?

In choosing between long forms and short forms, as we have discussed, there are many points to consider. Sometimes, as stated by industry professionals, all you need to know is your price point, assuming we have met our general standards for a DR product. However, price can mislead you to choose the wrong one.

Several years back I was working with a company on developing a weighted vest to help burn fat while basically just walking and doing everyday chores. This vest was designed to be fashionable and functional. It had slots to insert weight bars that would surround your body such that just simply wearing the vest and going about your day as you normally would, you would burn away additional fat due to the extra weight you were carrying.

As my client was able to get the vest produced at a price that allowed it to retail for two easy payments of $19.99, we had chosen the short-form route. Big mistake.

(continued)

Though the phones rang, the orders did not come in. Our feedback from our sales reps taught us that there was a strong interest in the product, but people were confused as to how it worked and what it actually did. We learned that what it really needed was a long-form format to provide the necessary time to explain the product, build product value, and emphasize the product's uniqueness. The short form gave us only enough time to make a few product claims—for example, that the vest was easy to use and would help the wearer lose weight fast and burn away extra fat just by wearing it—and then our call to action (CTA) to "buy it now!"

Lessons: When choosing between the long and short forms, there is a lot more to consider than just price. Choose the format that will allow you enough time to tell your product story, and if you can't tell it in the short-form infomercial, then don't use it. Use your customer feedback to understand your mistakes, learn from them, correct them, and move forward.

KEY CONCEPTS TO REMEMBER

1. There are two basic formats of infomercials:
(1) Short form (2 minutes)
(2) Long form (28.5 minutes)

2. There are three types of short-form commercials from an advertising perspective:
(1) The sale
(2) The lead generator
(3) The brand builder

3. The short form is great for lower-priced products—those priced from $14.99 to $39.99.

4. Short-form spots are relatively inexpensive to produce.

5. Short-form spots are more easily placed in the media on a broad scale.

6. Short-form spots are great for raising product awareness and support for already existing retail products.

7. Long forms provide the ability to connect you on many levels with your customers.

8. Long forms provide you with sufficient time to tell your product story, and they are great venues for introducing new technology.

9. Long forms provide you with sufficient time to reinforce the product's value proposition.

10. Long forms provide you with sufficient time to establish an emotional connection between your product and your potential customers.

11. Short forms are less risky from a dollar perspective because the cost of entry is low.

12. Long forms can be cost prohibitive because they are very expensive to produce and to buy media time in which to air them. This means that the long-form infomercial may be aired less frequently than the short-form infomercial would be. Thus it could take a longer time to truly test your show and build an audience.

8

Alternative Methods of DR Marketing

Home Shopping Channels and More

With the understanding and knowledge we have gained from the previous chapters, we can now explore other opportunities for selling. These opportunities are great adjuncts to infomercial selling, and they can also serve as stand-alone opportunities. They provide less expensive routes to bring your product to the consumer, and provide a way to build a brand and a business at the same time.

When going these routes, you will meet many, many people like you who have achieved great success with their products and who can share stories with you about how they were in the same place only a short time earlier.

HOME SHOPPING CHANNELS

The first option I want you to consider is to approach the television shopping networks like HSN, QVC, and ShopNBC. These venues serve as great alternatives to the infomercial approach. Many products that are not necessarily right for infomercials are a perfect fit for the shopping channels.

Advice from the Pros

Products that are successful on home shopping TV are not always successful in DR TV. However, a successful infomercial product has a great chance of success on a home shopping channel.

—Marcia Waldorf, partner and producer, Waldorf Crawford LLC

There are several reasons that this venue works well for a new inventor. One is that it is a great testing ground for a new product due to the low-cost barrier of entry compared to that of the infomercial. In addition, the home shopping TV programs feature products by category or "segment" (that is, the cooking segment, the do-it-yourself segment, and others), which gives you a better opportunity to present your product to your actual customers (as opposed to trying to catch their attention as they happen to flip the channel past your infomercial).

Advice from the Pros

Home shopping customers watch because, in their heart of hearts, they want to buy something, and they often have developed what they perceive to be a "relationship" with a show host. This means that they are, in essence, the perfect audience for a sales presentation. Because infomercials are not scheduled programming, most viewers happen upon them by chance while channel surfing. A potential viewer's disposition for buying products is not prelubricated.

—Marcia Waldorf, partner and producer, Waldorf Crawford LLC

Also, these channels are very open to working with new inventors. You can simply go to their Web sites and view information on the process. Each one welcomes new inventors with open arms.

Advice from the Pros

Some products are a natural for home shopping networks. I recommend home shopping for products that have mostly a female market and fit into their categories such as makeup, self-tanners, vitamins, clothes, and jewelry.

—Tara Borakos, president, Tara Productions, Inc.

These are the top three shopping channels (in no particular order):

1. *QVC, www.qvc.com.* Once at their home page, go to the bottom of the page and click on "corporate"; then on that page, click "QVC product search."

2. *HSN, www.hsn.com.* On their site, right on the bottom of the page is a link "become a vendor"; simply click on that for their information.

3. *ShopNBC, www.shopnbc.com.* They keep it simple as well with their "be a vendor" at the bottom of their home page.

Once at their Web sites, you may want to research more about the needs of these networks. ShopNBC, for instance, describes themselves and the new vendor opportunities as follows:

Who is ShopNBC?

As an upscale shopping network, ShopNBC promotes a wide variety of product categories to its customers, who are primarily affluent, sophisticated, and loyal shoppers. . . . ShopNBC programming is broadcast into approximately 60 million cable and satellite households. . . .

Which vendors make good candidates for ShopNBC?

Vendors who have products that demonstrate well, are unique, and have differentiating characteristics make good candidates for selling products on ShopNBC. Potential vendor products should also be new and exclusive, as well as need an introduction to the retail marketplace. In addition, products should appeal to not just ShopNBC's viewers but also to a broad audience.

These descriptions and perspectives pretty much hold true for QVC and HSN as well. Though they each take a slightly different perspective on product offerings and presentation, they all target a similar market base. Across the board, you will find their approach to attracting new vendors for new products to be open and very user friendly.

Something I strongly recommend in approaching this market is to identify a sales representative that currently works with these channels to help you through the process. Sales representatives are invaluable in terms of providing assistance and guidance in this area.

Advice from the Pros

When approaching the shopping channels, use a trusted and qualified representative, and don't do it yourself.
—Wendi W. Cooper, founder and CEO, C Spot Run Productions LLC

WHAT YOUR COSTS WILL BE

The negative aspect of going the home shopping route is that, if the shopping channels like your product, your product will have to be tested, viable, and ready to be manufactured. And if they approve your product "to air," be prepared to go into production quickly. In terms of quantities that you will need for an "airing," the show producers generally expect to generate about $5,000 to $10,000 per minute in an eight-minute segment (the usual length of the airtime granted for a product). If we approximate that at about $7,000 per minute ($56,000 total) and your invention is selling at $40, you would need to have at least 1,400 units from your manufacturer ready for air, at a purchase price of $18 (see below for further explanation). At a cost of goods of approximately $12, your initial investment in inventory would be about $16,800.

With your having the buyer's belief in the product, this monetary commitment is a relatively safe investment. However, there are many issues to consider.

First, the lower the number of units needed by you from your manufacturer, the more that manufacturer is going to charge you per unit to produce your product. This will cut into your profits, as you can't simply raise the wholesale price and the channels generally expect a 55 percent margin. That is, on a $40 item, the channel expects to profit at least $22 (or purchase your product for $18). The product selling pricing will be set based on the cost that you sell to them, but there is also the perceived value as compared to similar items in your category. So though you may pay more initially from your manufacturer, you may not be able to pass along that higher cost to the shopping channel, and thus you will be forced to make less on your initial run. The good news is, if it sells well and they reorder, you will be able to gain more favorable pricing from your supplier due to your increased volume. So in exchange for keeping your price low for the consumer and giving up a little profit up front, you end up making more in the end from building a product that sells.

The process can take some time, so be patient.

Advice from the Pros

From the buyer's accepting your product to its actual airing, the process can take between 3 and 12 months—and sometimes longer.

—Wendi W. Cooper, founder and CEO, C Spot Run Productions LLC

GETTING HELP

For help in this area there are many experts available to you who specialize in selling to these TV network accounts, and these experts are the sales representatives I referred to above. They not only have relationships with the buyers, but they also have a complete understanding of the process. In many cases they were buyers themselves or sold on air at one time or another. They act as sales representatives on your behalf, and they are paid based on your success. If they do not sell your product, they do not make money. Do not hire anyone who wants money up front to sell your product, but do hire an expert with a proven track record who works on a commission basis. Check the representative's track record, ask questions, and ask him or her about the products that are currently featured on these channels. The representative's success will speak for itself.

Typically, sales representatives for start-up companies or for new products get anywhere from 10 to 15 percent of your wholesale selling price—the price at which you sell your product to the shopping channel. They get paid only when you ship the product and have been paid by that account. Their services are invaluable because they not only help you sell your product, but they also help you with positioning, pricing, and in some cases even manufacturing. For extra services they may charge a consulting fee, which, for the added value, is worth paying. But understand and be clear what you're getting for your money and insist on performance on all counts. Last but certainly not least, the seasoned sales representative in this area can even help in getting you "good" airtime, which is time on air during a product segment that fits with your product and during an hour that is highly watched. There are no guarantees, but to have an experienced advocate on your side will certainly go a long way.

Once the buyer expresses an interest in your product and decides to move forward, you will have to submit a sample of your product for quality assurance (QA) testing. If it's approved and when it's approved, the shopping channel will give you a purchase order (PO) and begin discussing positioning and airtime with you.

Advice from the Pros

It is best to have a fully developed, finished product when presenting to buyers. Why? Because everyone has an opinion and a creative vision, so don't leave your item open for scrutiny.

—Wendi W. Cooper, founder and CEO, C Spot Run Productions LLC

OTHER KEY ISSUES

Keep in mind that the shopping channel will return to you any units it doesn't sell. This means that if only half of your 1,400 units sell, you will not get paid for 700 of them, and you may need to find another selling venue for them. If the *sell-through* of a new item is within the range of the per-minute needs, or if sales spike on your item as compared to the others offered in that hour, there is a good chance you'll have earned a second airing.

Another issue is that since you are a new inventor with a new product, it's very possible that you and your product will be put on late at night; this is an aspect you've no control over. But that's okay because, as stated above, your product sales will be compared to those in the same hour, and, if you do well, the shopping channel will work to find better and better times, until there is no such thing as a bad time for your product—or until it just stops selling.

If you have gone it alone and you have found a buyer at a shopping channel on your own, and now you want to go further but you do not fully understand the ins and outs of working with a shopping channel, you may want to ask the contact you are working with (we're going to assume the shopping channel is very interested in your product and you now *have* a contact at one of these channels) if he or she can recommend a sales representative who can help you. The sales representatives generally work on a commission basis, and they will know and can teach you the language and processes of the home shopping industry as well. You can also read industry publications like *Response* magazine or check with the Electronic Retailing Association (ERA, www.retailing.org), and both of these sources can give you good leads on finding representatives and many other industry professionals.

THE DOWNSIDE OF HOME SHOPPING CHANNELS

If you are successful with the home shopping route, you should consider the other DR marketing avenues. Using only a home shopping channel may limit your product to a narrow audience because you have a limited group watching these channels and get limited selling time. Compare that to an infomercial on several stations in different markets, which will give you more coverage of a broader audience—but take it one step at a time, go slowly, and prove your product's sales viability so that then you can make the most of both venues.

There are some other negatives to the home shopping option: Your item is on TV for a limited time, and, until you are established, it may not be seen again for weeks. Also, you are limited to the on-air talent already available at these channels, whereas you can choose your own presenters for an infomercial. You can also choose how your product is positioned in an infomercial, and while all of the home shopping channels are of course going to try to sell as many units as they can, they have a specific way of doing things, and you may find a way that works better for your product in the infomercial route. (For statistics on home shopping customers versus infomercial customers, see Appendix H.)

However, if your product gains a strong following on television, going into broader distribution through national retail outlets—like Wal-Mart or Sears—is a possibility, and that is the best approach for both success and longevity for your product.

DR MARKETING ON THE WEB

The Web is a component of DR TV, and it's a handy tool that can be used in catching the attention of millions of people. With tools like streaming video or *Flash* animation, you can demonstrate your product online. Or if you've created an infomercial but are not ready to commit to ad space on television, you can show either portions of it or all of it on the Internet.

You can create a compelling Web site through which consumers may purchase your product. Then use e-mail campaigns, sign up with Web search engines, and advertise on other people's Web sites using banner ads and other online ad placements to generate word-of-mouth interest in your product and get people to click through to your Web site to find your product. I recommend either doing some Internet research or talking to a small boutique ad agency that specializes in Web advertising to help with this.

The problem with the Web is reaching your audience. There are millions of Web sites. There are probably hundreds of thousands of shopping sites. Betting on your audience's coming to you when they type in "gardening utensils" could be a long shot. However, as an adjunct to a DR TV campaign, the Web can be a tremendous asset and a good way to build revenues incrementally. It provides a place for those who have seen your product on TV to go and look at it for a longer period of time, study it, and consider it and reconsider it prior to purchasing it. These additional sales can amount to as much as 25 percent of your DR sales in conjunction with a successful TV campaign, adding tremendously to your profit margin.

GRASSROOTS OPTIONS

The grassroots approach is another good one. But it can be a slow process. You could start off by selling to friends and family or to the public at local school events or other area events where products can be sold (street fairs, community functions, and so on). From there you can even go to the local stores in your area—the convenience stores, hardware stores, or even the grocery stores.

With this approach you start by selling a few units in these venues, which would prove that the item can sell. After that, you start expanding your circle. Take your success stories to other retailers and begin to expand your selling circle to larger, more regional chains or even to the local stores of a national chain. There are also occasions when the local store manager of a large national chain may be allowed to buy a product on limited basis for that manager's store only. All of this helps build your program and helps you gain visibility.

With the successes from these venues and some good word-of-mouth interest, you build a following. Then you continue your grassroots approach by expanding on your local following through added visibility. Contact magazines, and send samples to those magazines whose coverage relates well to your product. This all can help generate a buzz. Many publications, from *Parents* to *BusinessWeek,* are always interested in new hot items.

At this point, you have hopefully enjoyed some sales and may have even built up some extra funds with which to advertise your product on local radio. Or your success stories may be strong enough for you to now sell your product to the major retailers. Once that happens, you don't have to worry as much about the ad campaign (although it's always good to support your retail presence with your own advertising campaign when you can, as the retailers take those campaigns into consideration when evaluating your product for consideration to purchase) because you will gain great visibility from the mere fact that your product is in one of these national retail stores. Who knows, maybe they'll place your product in their circulars (that is, store publications that advertise products and are circulated in all of their stores and local and national newspapers).

The process of selling to national and large regional retailers is much more complicated, and I have oversimplified it for the purpose of illustrating the growth pattern of a roll-out of this sort. A successful grassroots campaign can take three to five years to roll out to a broad national scale product offering. And, as with everything else we've discussed, there just aren't any guarantees it will succeed in the long term. When you do get to the stage of selling to the larger retail chains, you will want to contact and consider hiring a professional, a sales representative. The representative doesn't just help you sell your product, but also helps you through the process and explains all that you will need to know in order to go in this direction, just as we described above for your dealing with the shopping channels.

Using a grassroots marketing strategy can prove fruitful over the long run, and to take this journey it is required that you know a few things . . .

At the beginning of the grassroots stage, you will need a fully functional working product and a sample of it to show when you approach that first mom-and-pop store, or even if you want to present it to friends for purposes of purchasing and trying your product. Be ready and able to ship actual products in the event that you do get a small order from the mom-and-pop stores or if your circle of friends are interested. You will need the finished product packaged as if it were being sold in retail stores nationwide—obviously, the packaging would be more important for the stores than for your friends. You will need to make sure any and all safety and legal issues concerning your product are anticipated and dealt with. There are a lot of details to tend to as you go through the stages of development—patents, market research, and so on. Check other products in your categories, see the claims they are making, and consult a friend or attorney for advice in this regard. But don't let these tasks overwhelm you—though there are a lot of them, they do have a way of falling into place.

Another advantage of the grassroots approach is that if you're successful at the local stores and if that success is sufficient to prove the viability of your product at the consumer level, you will have created several options as to what to do next:

1. Continue to build sales through a slow expansion of your circle of buyers from among your friends and the local stores.

2. Take your immediate success stories and aim higher at the larger retail outlets and work your way toward a giant like Target or Wal-Mart.

3. Follow the path from the above example "Cutting through DR Using a Scissor for Salads" and build your path to success from the shopping channels.

4. License your product to a large DR marketing company based upon your localized success.

The fact is, no one knows if an item will sell until it is seen by a consumer and that consumer makes a decision as to whether or not to buy that product. The grassroots approach to marketing and distributing a product through a local market, if successful, can help an inventor by providing proven sales data that can be used in selling the product to the bigger retailers. The sales record can also help the inventor obtain the support of sales representatives or a license from a large marketing company. (See Figure 8–1.)

Another consideration in choosing how to market your first product is to consider a company that can help you along the way. Sometimes the inventor needs to allow the lawyers to be lawyers, allow the marketers to be marketers and, well, the inventors to be inventors. There is no need to try to do everything yourself when there are many companies out there that are quite good at handling the various processes and helping you accomplish the many tasks along the path to success. Also, don't be afraid to license, sell off, or otherwise partner with a company. At the end of the day, licensing could be the most profitable approach for you because going it alone can and will cost a great deal, and in either case the end results are not guaranteed, and a license is a good hedge from the beginning.

I don't want you to believe that following this dream on your own won't cost a lot of money (it will), and I would not recommend mortgaging the house, betting the farm, or selling the kids to achieve

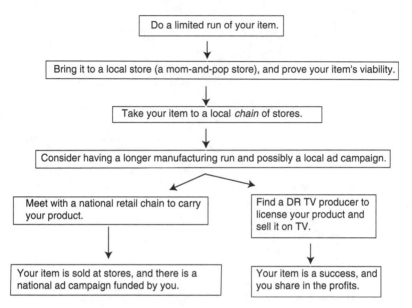

Figure 8–1   The Successful Grassroots Tree

it—but do go after it with all of your heart. Thus, keep in mind that through licensing, you can still get rich, very rich . . . and have time for family and friends, or to invent more million-dollar winners.

There are many viable ways for you to approach the market—from concept to manufacturing to selling—cost effectively. Licensing your first product is one of those potentially profitable methods.

If you have established a successful grassroots program for your product, it will give you negotiating leverage with potential licensees (the DR marketing companies), which will allow you to possibly make more on the initial licensing fee as well as achieve a higher royalty amount (the percentage you earn from each unit sold, which averages at about 2 to 5 percent).

Licensing may also be a great introduction for you as a newcomer into the world of DR TV marketing, and the next time around, you may be able to produce your spot yourself.

 ## Direct Response Marketing Success Story

Cutting through DR Using a Scissor for Salads

The creators of the Toss & Chop created it, designed it, and presented it to QVC.

QVC bought in, and the product was an immediate success, selling a tremendous number of units in its first airing.

With the product's success, several DR companies approached the inventors, offering to take their product to the public through a DR TV campaign. But the inventors, though open to the idea, ultimately preferred to stick with QVC and go directly to retail from there, and all on their own.

Of course, when those DR companies were turned down, they decided—since they could not license the product—to enter the kitchen utensil category for chopping and tossing salads on their own. And, though they were able to do so because the category is not protected, the inventors had a great advantage: Their product was protected. They had their patent, and as we stressed the importance of in Chapter 4, it was a well-written one. They were able to stop most of these companies from entrenching upon this product's category and in particular its original concept and functionality.

By taking their time to develop and market the product—and bringing the product to market not based on a particular selling season but simply when it was ready, they made sure they were covered in all regards: from a well-written patent to a fully developed product. They even went as far as creating a less expensive version of their own product (the "knockoff"). They were methodical in their approach, and they stopped at every stage to look and see where they were at, and they explored their options before going forward. They are a textbook example of how individuals can create, design, develop, and market their own products. Their execution was near-perfect, and their results were stellar.

Their approach is one to follow, but if you do not have or cannot arrange to have the financial resources to go the distance, then at the point where they turned down the offers from other companies, you should not. If you get the offers, get several, compare them, ne-

(*continued*)

gotiate your best deal, and license your product—the financial rewards will be great!

So take your time, and go at each step with caution and care, consider all your options, and understand what you can and can't do—and, most important, don't try to circumvent the process. That is, don't cut (or toss and chop) corners.

Lessons:

Shopping channels can be great for launching new products because they are open to ideas and first-time inventors

Though shopping channels appear to be a less expensive way to market a new invention, in reality, they aren't less expensive. There is no cheap and easy way to launch a new product. But if you can afford the investment in using the shopping channel venues, the returns can be great.

Once again, beware, and be aware, of competition!

KEY CONCEPTS TO REMEMBER

1. Shopping channels are a great venue for introducing new products because they are open to working with first-time inventors and they welcome new products with open arms.

2. Make sure your product is fully developed and ready to present to the shopping channels. Though they are open to working with new inventions, they want to see fully developed and ready-to-market products.

3. Use the professionals. Sales representatives and consultants for the shopping channels can be worth their weight in gold. But keep you eyes open, and pay only for results.

4. If you are selling the product yourself, make sure you will be able to ship the product when promised and that you have covered all of your product's safety and legal issues.

5. The Web itself is a quick, easy, first approach to a market; however, with all of the clutter now on the Internet, it is hard to catch the eye of a prospective customer and truly build sales volume through this method alone.

6. The Web will provide a great venue for you to tell your story and build some customer loyalty. This potential following of customers will serve you well as you expand your program to TV or retail or to licensing your product.

7. The Web is truly a productive adjunct to a DR TV campaign, providing potential customers a place to go to spend some time with your product and understand it better prior to customers' making their purchase.

8. The grassroots approach to marketing is great for all of those who want to take it a bit slower. With patience and determination, you can use the Internet venue to remain in control and have time to expand at a rate you are comfortable with.

9. The grassroots approach can provide you with localized success stories that will help you during each round of expansion while giving you time to tweak your marketing and sales efforts at very little cost.

10. Using a grassroots marketing campaign, you will have a cost-effective approach to small markets. You will also be able to retain proportionately more profits as compared with using other approaches to marketing.

11. Do not be afraid to let go. It's okay, and most times it's beneficial, to sell or license your first product to a company already in the business.

9

Creating an Infomercial
and Getting It Aired

HOW AN INFOMERCIAL IS MADE

At this point you are, most likely, comfortable with your role as Inventor (yes, with a capital "I"). You have a firm hold of your product, and you know its strengths and perhaps how it should be positioned to consumers. But you're not 100 percent comfortable with the world of DR TV. That feels so distant, hard to grasp, and even just a bit more complex than you had anticipated.

Not to fear; this chapter is where we break down the making of the infomercial. By the end of this chapter you'll be, well, not quite an expert, but not a fish out of water either. Perhaps a fish in new, fresh waters may be the best analogy.

Keep in mind that you will not be producing the infomercial yourself. Maybe you've been to a local film festival in your town, watched a special on TV, or heard all about people making movies themselves, and you're thinking, "Well, why can't I just get my video camera, a few friends, and make a commercial in my kitchen (or workout room or garage workshop)?" Okay, you *can*, but I do *not* recommend this plan of action if you want to be successful.

DR marketing companies and producers who have infomercial experience understand how to navigate through these worlds. They know how to position your product and they know what audiences will respond to. They've likely seen great products fail and mediocre products succeed, and they understand why this happened. They know the nuances and needs of DR marketing. As it was stated previously, you be the inventor and let the others do the things they do best.

Advice from the Pros

Experience and diligence are the two greatest benefits that an agency can provide to a marketer. DR is unique, and success is dependent on so many factors.

—Dick Weschler, president and CEO, Lockard & Weschler Direct, media buying agency

Also, the monetary investment in creating an infomercial is no small step. But if you do know people in the business and maybe even have some experience filming, then by all means give it a shot, but not for the actual infomercial. Instead, use anything you film to have some footage on hand to present potential investors, DR marketing companies, and other potential licensees, or QVC and the like. Again, use only a professional producer who is well versed in infomercials for your production.

PEOPLE INVOLVED IN THE INFOMERCIAL PRODUCTION

So let's look at the types of companies and individuals involved with this part of the process and what each does:

A DR marketing company will be responsible for all costs necessary to arrange manufacturing, warehousing and distribution; media buying; telemarketing; fulfillment; and customer service as well as sales to retail outlets. The marketing company will set up a Web site and any and everything else needed relating to the sales of your product; this also includes creating the offer, determining the selling price of your product, and choosing the additional product or products that will be featured as the give-away in the commercial as well as those sold with your main product through your telemarketing. Such add-on features might be a deluxe version or additional products such as carrying cases, chargers, and warranties. These additional products are commonly referred to as the *up-sells*.

A TV production company will produce the commercial, write the script, hire the talent, and develop the means by which the product is presented.

You will find that the DR marketing companies each have a favorite production company or two that they go to, and conversely, the TV production companies who work in DR will always be able to recommend a DR marketing group.

In all cases, from your marketing companies to the media buying companies to your production companies, the industry is segmented by specialty. Some production companies specialize in the fitness category, others in housewares or skin care. Some marketing companies are best at household products while others are best at fitness. Some media buying companies focus on national cable buys while others focus on syndication ad buys, or they focus on short form (two-minute spots) versus long form. Whichever field, and whatever company you choose, be certain to look at the products and companies they have been involved with, and check that they are in good financial health as a company.

Advice from the Pros

When hiring a producer for a long-form show or short-form spot, be sure to look at the track record of the producer. Make sure the producer has had success in the same category.
—Tara Borakos, president, Tara Productions, Inc.

And, most important, do *not* pay for a marketing company to market your product. A trustworthy marketing company will pay you, either up front or in the form of royalties on future sales. (The *service companies*—those providing you with services such as setting up your phone number and giving you phone support—operate differently, and you may have to pay them an advance, or a deposit, toward services. This is standard procedure for any service company when conducting business with a new entity.) But what it always comes down to is that you need to feel comfortable with whomever it is you are working with, and it's your gut that will probably be your best guide. And if you do heed the suggestion to license your first product, then refer to Appendix A for additional information on licensing and what to expect if you choose to go this route.

Before you begin your search and approach that TV production company to have that infomercial or two-minute spot produced, be certain to have a few things in place:

1. ***Have your product ready to go.*** It can be a prototype, but it must work like, and *look* like, what the final product will actually be.

2. ***Have your product protected and your company ready to go.*** This doesn't include just patents (pending or issued) but also the setting up of a corporate entity. For this purpose, either a *limited liability company* (LLC) or a *Subchapter S corporation* works well (consult your attorney and/or accountant on which is best for you). Create a good name for your prod-

uct, then file for your trademark. Conduct some research on trademarks because certain forms of words and phrases are not able to be trademarked. Have these papers filed and finished.

3. *Make certain that you have determined your target market.*

4. *Identify your product's unique selling proposition (USP).*

With the above in place, the first step to producing your commercial is to hire a production company specializing in infomercials and DR marketing. As mentioned previously, a great resource for finding the right company is the Electronic Retailing Association (www.retailing.org). The production company will identify shooting locations—determining whether you'll be shooting on a set or, for instance, at a local mall—find your talent, whether that be a celebrity, a respected physician, or just a good host, and gather your crew. Your crew includes the people who work the lighting, cameras, and other equipment, those who design the set, prepare the props, and do the hair and makeup, and so forth. This company will also handle any contracts and negotiations with any talent and subcontractors that are needed. When looking for a production company, be thorough before hiring. Speak with more than one company, and look at recent products they have produced shows for and the shows themselves. Find a fit based on category fit, product success, and recommendations. Keep in mind personality as well, as you need to be comfortable with whom you work. And don't forget to check their references. Bottom line: Do your homework.

As you know, there are two forms of infomercials.

The short form will cost in the $25,000 to $50,000 range while the long-form commercial will cost in the area of $150,000 to $300,000, which will include the producer, the script, the actors, the locations, the sets, props, lighting, sound, and so on. Again, let me stress, mortgaging the house and selling all of your belongings on eBay to raise the money is not recommended. Sure, you can take a page out of the "independent film" book and ask friends, family, and associates if they want to back a venture of this nature, but you *must* let them know the following:

1. They too should not invest anything beyond their means or any amount that could potentially cause financial harm to them should the venture not work.

2. It is possible, no matter how amazing your product is perceived to be (as perception is everything when raising money in early-stage development) that they may not ever get this investment back. No one can predict the future, and sales are never guaranteed.

Advice from the Pros

We believe that losses should be cut aggressively. You can usually identify a campaign that isn't going to make it within a few days.

—Dick Weschler, president and CEO, Lockard & Weschler Direct, media buying agency

When you are in the process of hiring a producer, know that most will not take on a product they do not believe has a chance to make it in the DR business. The reason for this is that what they charge to produce the infomercial, or spot, is a small amount of money relative to the general marketplace for traditional advertising (see below). Instead, the infomercial production company will make their money on the success of your product because they are also paid a percentage of sales (typically 1 to 1.5 percent). Thus, their real profit, if any, will be made on the upside—the sales.

Advice from the Pros

We will turn down a product that we feel won't be successful. We have a limited amount of time so we don't want to waste anyone's time or money.

—Tara Borakos, president, Tara Productions, Inc.

In the world of media production, $25,000 to $50,000 for a one-day shoot (short-form spot), or $150,000 to $300,000 for a two or three day plus possible weeks for prep (long form) is not a great deal of money when compared to the typical 30-second TV commercial for which the cost of production *begins* at $300,000.

From scripts to staff, and staging to stage crew, a lot of the money you pay the production company goes back out to pay for those that they hire. Again, producers will make their real money only if your product is a success.

GETTING STARTED

To begin the production process, the producer will start by setting up a shoot schedule and putting together the entire plan of what you need. Prep time is about four to six weeks, but it could be more depending on whether your infomercial is short form or long form. The producer usually has sets (preconstructed settings such as a kitchen, living room, workshop, or gym) readily available or knows of places to shoot that fit your product (the on-location shots such as the beach, a boat, in a pool, or at a salon). But he or she will need time to write the script, secure the talent, gather the testimonials, and get the necessary staff and location together.

After the producer has coordinated the basic schedule, the following will need to be accomplished:

1. Determine product positioning, or selling point, based on its USP, as well as the selling price(s) for the product.

2. Prepare the script.

3. Get the product ready for testimonials based on objectives for marketing.

4. Arrange for the testing of the product by testimonial participants.

5. Determine a spokesperson, if needed.

6. Scout for other participating talent to appear in the show or spot.

7. Plan sets, props, locations, and so on.

8. Coordinate all elements for shoot date(s).

9. Set up a shoot schedule.

10. Shoot the show.

THE SCRIPT

For the script, you should work closely with your producer. He or she will provide the basic ideas, taking into consideration your input and passion, in order to help formulate all elements of the script. The format is pretty standard: Show problem, show solution, explain the "secret," provide testimonial to support the solution, give value proposition, make offer, and close sale. (See the script from my Smart Tape presentation in Appendix C.)

Whether you produce a 2-minute or a 30-minute show, the basic formula holds. The format may vary slightly, but the basic elements remain the same.

After the script is ready, you will then of course need your product to be ready to be tested and shot for the show. You will either have hand-made samples or actual preproduction samples from a small run your manufacturer has produced for you. You will need several for both the actual production of the show and the testimonials.

THE TESTIMONIALS

Advice from the Pros

While the product is the *heart* of the infomercial, testimonials are the *heartbeat*. They must be *natural*, *real*, and *passionate*.

—Marcia Waldorf, partner and producer, Waldorf Crawford LLC

Besides coordinating all of the above aspects, the producer will also train people to demonstrate your item, and demonstrate it well. The producer will also obtain the testimonials—that is, those people who look into the camera and say, "I tried this product, and it worked for me." They can be from people you know who have tried and liked your product or sometimes they *are* just testimonial actors, simply because an actor knows how to hit the lines just right. But the fact that they are actors does not mean they are not familiar with the product. In all cases, they have tried the product and sometimes even lived with the product for a certain period of time.

Organizing the testimonial is your producer's job, and he or she may also go to consumer marketing companies or even talent agencies and utilize test groups. The product may be tested for a few minutes, an entire day, or several weeks depending on your product. For instance, a can opener can take minutes; a fishing reel, an entire day; a fitness or diet aid, several weeks. Your producer will handle all of this, and he or she will make sure to get the best testimonials. The key to a great testimonial is to capture unscripted, natural enthusiastic reactions to your product.

One final note on testimonials: Within the testimonial, the producer will want to make sure he or she has captured those people whose experience coincides with the product claims. It is very im-

Advice from the Pros

Viewers viscerally *feel* when a testimonial is just speaking words, rather than expressing true feelings. We approach testimonials in a very personal way . . . and at close range, inviting viewers to see if the message in their eyes matches the words they speak.

—Marcia Waldorf, partner and producer, Waldorf Crawford LLC

portant that any and all claims that are made concerning your product are accurate and can be substantiated.

For example, if you claim within your infomercial that it slices and dices, "all this" in fewer than 10 seconds, it will be required that the 10 seconds or less can be substantiated. Thus, those people who experienced such results should be used both for the testimonial aspect of the show and to sign off on a document acknowledging their results. If with your item you can "lose five pounds in five days," make sure you have proven (scientific or clinical proofs are the best) studies to support and substantiate that type of claim, especially for weight-loss, vitamin, and diet products. Even with video recorded testimonials that concur with your product claims, you will need to back them up with documented support from those that achieved the results stated. In arranging for the testimonials, regardless of product category, your producer will help coordinate all of the necessary forms and documents for substantiation with those individuals that are participating in trying your product.

Though the perception of the consumer is that in many cases the claims made in infomercials are false, and though there are indeed a handful of unscrupulous companies that make false claims, most infomercials do not. What happens to the ones that do? The

Federal Trade Commission (FTC) is the governmental body that oversees this area, and you can be sure that not only will the commission shut those companies down but it will also make available for public scrutiny the documents supporting the commission's claims of fraud and fines for millions of dollars it levied against those companies that chose to lie, cheat, and steal. Bottom line: Make your claims, substantiate and prove your claims, and tout that proof through testimonial, but whatever you do, keep it truthful. Also, consult an attorney for "clearance" on any claims that you feature in your ads.

THE SHOOT

When the commercial is ready to shoot, you will get to participate— you will be invited "on set' to give input and discuss what you like or don't like. Again, this isn't a chance to take over. Be the inventor . . . but do share your thoughts and opinions. And, most important, share your passion!

Now that you understand the process, let's look at the long form versus the short form again. Though we covered the pros and cons in Chapter 7, let's look again at the differences but this time to gain an understanding of how those differences relate to production.

THE SHORT FORM

The two-minute spot is composed of the presentation, benefits, disclosure of the product's "magic," reiteration of its benefits with testimonials, building of the offer and the creation of value ("Normally this would sell for as much $100, but now . . ."), and the call to action ("Call now!"). Then the commercial will often "up the offer" to close the deal ("Not convinced of the value yet? Well, if you call right now, we'll also include . . .")—it's the *pièce de résistance*.

THE LONG FORM

One main reason to do a long-form commercial is that it gives you more time with your customer. More time with the potential buyers means more potential sales.

Also, if your highly demonstrable item can be used to solve many problems, the long form gives you a real chance to show that and create a story, or stories, around it. Those stories can be based on the idea of "Look at all the great ways to use this item" and/or "I had X problem(s), so one day, I invented Y!" The story allows you to emotionally connect with your consumers, to show them the benefits of your product and how it will positively affect their lives. The long form also allows you to make product comparisons. In a short-form commercial, it's not likely you'll have time to demonstrate *and* compare the product to others like it. Don't despair though; you can still build excitement around the product. Whichever format you choose, ideally the end result will be to compel the viewer to a "call to action" (CTA)—that is, the viewer will call to *buy* your product.

The long-form format is cut into segments:

1. There will be three 6- to 7-minute segments, wherein you share information about your product. They start out with an introduction by your host, who will explain your product and its benefits, which will then be shown to the viewer. Each of the three segments will talk about your product but usually with a slightly different approach or "angle."

2. There will be three CTA segments during the 28½-minute infomercial. Talk about the item, then present your offer (that is, show the price), reinforce your product's value, and have your giveaways here ("Plus your free flashlight set!"). The idea is to get people to act and to make that call. During these 2- to 3-minute segments, you can also drive people to your Web site, and, here's a great DR secret: Run your Web site address along the bottom of the screen throughout your commercial; that way, even the casual viewer, or remote-control

"flipper," can take note and possibly visit your site later. This strategy has proven to generate as much as 25 percent of TV sales. (See Appendix D for a sample CTA.)

Within the CTA in the long form, or within the last 15 seconds or so of the short form, is the end tag. The *end tag* is the place in the commercial where you show your complete product and all of its included premiums (the "offer"), state the price, and repeat the phone number to call. Don't forget to add, "But you must call now, operators are standing by!" The entire end tag is made in the postproduction period of the infomercial production process, or after your commercial is shot. The images of your product(s) are made on what is called a *blue screen*, so that the background can be changed digitally. This allows you to use different 1-800 numbers (so you know when orders come in, on which channel the callers viewed your ad), and to test different prices, offers, and different shipping and handling costs. Also, the voice-over used (the voice you hear announcing the number to call and the price) is done in postproduction as well.

One element that has not been mentioned is the postproduction, duplication, and distribution facility. This is the company that inserts the phone numbers and selling prices at the end of your commercial and even arranges for the voice-overs, or announcements, in your end tag. This company also supplies many other production and postproduction services. It then takes the completed tape of your commercial and makes duplicates of it with its individualized phone numbers so that you may track which stations the calls come in from. It then distributes the edited duplicates to their respective stations for airing.

There are many types of postproduction companies, but only a few are in the business of catering to the world of DR. One such company, Treehouse Media Services, will work with both large and small clients alike, and it will take the time to walk you through all stages of this important process.

At the beginning of the production process, the producer will ask you why your product is great, what makes it useful, and why do people need it. It's your product, and you should know the answers better than anyone else. Your answers will give the producer ideas for marketing strategies, and he or she and the DR marketing company (if licensed, if not you directly) will consider the best ways to position the product in each segment as well as consider how best to show its value.

Some of the strategies the producers will use include the utilization of catch phrases like "It's three tools in one!" or "the one tool that does it all!" or use a much stronger approach by adding a premium to the main offer such as a cheese grater, a flashlight, a bathrobe, or simply another one of the actual product ("we'll double your offer!")—the premium usually consists of something that already exists and has a low cost, but high perceived value and complements your product. Exclusive offers and premiums help enhance the perceived value of your item and thus the overall offer.

You *can* first test your product without any special additions or premiums. Make the commercial and run it for a week, testing your item at a price point of $39.99. If people aren't calling, it's for one of two reasons:

1. They don't feel the benefits of your product are there—that is, they don't feel the need for your product.

2. They feel your product is simply too expensive or the value is not there. This means you may have to lower the price point or offer more (or perhaps more enticing) add-ons.

Ultimately, what you need to ascertain is, are people not calling because of the price/value proposition or because of the product itself. We get into this subject further in the next chapter on assessing your results and explain in detail with actual reports.

If the initial response is weak, you can add premiums or lower your price. Of course, because this is the infomercial market, viewers have expectations because they have seen many infomercials over the years. So they are *expecting* premiums. They want that free set of steak knives.

Advice from the Pros

The product itself always remains supreme. If there is a discount of some sort included with the offer, there is no way of measuring whether or not that impacts the customer's decision to purchase. In many cases, however, a bonus item with a high perceived value has been more effective.

—Mike Sobo, president, SAS Group, DR marketing company

These premiums do add to the costs, but it's these things that make the offer more attractive and often compel people to call. So the extra outlay of $2 or $3 to add these items to your product offer can mean the difference between financial success and failure in terms of orders, and some of the costs related to these items can be offset by the profit margins obtained from an efficient shipping and handling campaign.

Keep in mind that when you sell an item at $39.99, you're also asking the consumer to add several dollars for shipping and handling. *Shipping* is, perhaps obviously, the actual shipping cost of the item. *Handling* is meant to cover the costs to pack, label, and ship the items as well as other related costs. The actual handling cost is determined by a number of factors and varies from product to product, as do shipping prices, but your shipping and handling price should more than cover these additional costs, and the income from this element could be a profit center when managed properly, and as mentioned, it can help defray some of those additional costs that arise from such add-ons and premiums.

A good fulfillment center can help you set up this pricing structure and provide you with all the necessary insights in terms of costs and volume shipping discounts and overall efficiencies with running your program. For a full list of fulfillment companies specializing in the informercial business, check out www.retailing.org.

Did you see it? This is the moment, your moment. When your commercial is ready to air, the chance to put your product out into the world for all to see, for the consumers to . . . consume! Now you have an invention, a commercial to promote your invention, and a team of people helping you to sell it. Will it be a success? How will you know? And what do you do next?

 ### Direct Response Marketing Success Story

The "Smart Tape" and "Smart" Licensing Deal

Though I have become well versed in product manufacturing and distribution, I have also learned my limitations. Within the DR business, one of the first products that I completely designed and developed myself was the Smart Tape. Though I knew I could manufacture the product and I knew my way around the production side of the short form, I still deferred to the experts in the end.

I had researched my category, developed my product fully, and had a working prototype in hand. I had done a preliminary trademark search on the name, and I was clear to go in terms of having all the necessary intellectual property protection for the product itself. As the product would sell for $19.99, I chose to go with a short-form format. I hired a producer and put in place all of the elements I needed to be ready to produce and then test my commercial.

And so I did it. The commercial was produced, and the tape was sent to the postproduction company to add in the visual cues for the price and the mailing address and to add the voice-over for the ". . . all for only $19.99, but you must call now!" and of course the actual phone number to call.

And did they call. A great success. But now what? Do I run it myself, or do I sell, or license it to another company.

(continued)

Yes, even I chose to license my product to another company. A company that was already achieving success in the hardware category with DR TV products. Why? Because I was not set up for sales and distribution at that time. Yes, I outsourced the production of the commercial, as well as the media buying, the warehousing for the initial product inventory, the telemarketing, and customer service. But to carry this program and drive it to a level of true success, I needed more. I need a company with enough money to fund an ongoing commercial, handle importing and warehousing on much greater level, and control and set up proper distribution to the major retail stores.

A partnership deal was struck, and the partner took over the commercial and immediately began to distribute to retail. Because of their company size and presence in the market, the partner was able to begin to get orders immediately from retailers so it began shipping as many as 40,000 units per month in short order.

Lessons:

1. Even the seasoned professional needs to know his or her limitations. Know what you do best and what you don't.

2. Do not be afraid to partner, license, or sell your product to another company because there are many advantages to such arrangements.

3. There are economies of scale and speed to market that others already in the market bring to the table that a newcomer could never have.

KEY CONCEPTS TO REMEMBER

1. There are several elements needed to get your infomercial produced and aired.

2. Hire only an expert within the DR business to produce your infomercial—only an experienced producer will truly understand how to make your infomercial successful.

3. Work closely with the producer, and share your thoughts and perspectives—after all you are the inventor.

4. Have your product ready to go. Make sure you have covered yourself on all legal issues.

5. Understand who your target market is and what your USP is.

6. Choose a producer based on some good research and recommendations. Look at the producer's successes as well as failures.

7. Make sure you can work with the producer on a personal level. His or her attitude toward you will be reflected in his or her efforts in making your infomercial.

8. Work closely on the script. Heed the producer's advice, but ensure that your product message is coming across.

9. Work hard at capturing the best testimonials for your product. They are key to your success. They must be truthful and sincere and substantiated.

10. Know your product, understand your product, and work closely with your producer so he or she can convey the essential benefits of the product.

11. Test your product at a few different price points with a couple of different premiums.

12. In licensing or selling your product to a marketing company, never pay a marketing company to take your product—no matter what it promises. If a marketing company believes in your product, it will pay you, either up front or in royalties on the back end.

10

Selling and Analyzing the Results

You did it!

Your commercial is ready, your product waits in the wings, and you've got your eye on that convertible (the college tuition for junior can wait). So what happens next?

START WITH A TELEMARKETING SCRIPT

The next element you need in place is your telemarketing. The telemarketing company is where you get your *operators*. The telemarketing company operators will be answering the calls that come in from the 1-800 numbers located at the bottom of the screen, and they will process your orders. The way they answer the phone is extremely important—the operators will be following a script from the moment they pick up the phone. They are the voice of your company.

The script for your answering service will shape the voice of your company, and what the operators say and how they say it will determine if the customer calling you will buy. Through the analysis of your product and the up-sells you will include with it, a telemarketing script will have to be created to make certain everything is covered appropriately.

Any question a consumer has about your product will most likely be covered in the script. In addition, operators will have information about the product that duplicates what viewers saw in the commercial. The operators will also have shipping information and additional offers to make (for example, "Would you like expedited shipping for only $10 more?" or "Would you like to order two and receive the free cookbook?"). I have included as Appendix E a sample from the Smart Tape telemarketing sales script. This appendix shows a fairly typical script from the operator's greeting to the close or sale. It also includes the product information and shows how the up-sell is executed in its most basic form.

There are many telemarketing companies available in the marketplace; however, there are only a handful that are well known within the DR industry. These companies can be found advertised or listed in *Response* magazine or through the Electronic Retailing Association. These companies offer services in all aspects of telemarketing. They will help with everything from writing the script with you to working with you determine the type of service you need, from live operators answering your calls to automated voice response set-ups that have prerecorded voice prompts to walk the caller through the

Advice from the Pros

Order a few products yourself, and don't play "trick the operator." Just order as you would any other product and listen to the scripting. If you have questions, see how the operator answers your queries and how long it takes for the operator to find your answer. Call for both short-form and long-form products.

—Kimberly Fairfield-Frieders, director, sales, West Corporation, telemarketing company ordering process (also known as IVR interactive voice response). Which one is right for you depends on the program and several factors. The sales representative at the telemarketing company will walk you through both and help you with that decision.

PUT THE PRODUCT TO THE TEST

With your show in hand and your telemarketing company and script in place, you are then ready to go live to the media test.

This is your big day when you put your product to the test. Your show will get placed on air in front of the buying public. How you do this and what stations or channels your show goes on is determined by the experts: the media buyers. These experts in the media buying category will buy, or "place," the media, meaning that they will determine where your ad or show should run and contact the stations to determine what airtime is available, on what days and at what time, and they will buy based on what's best for your product, or what they feel might be best.

The way media buyers find your time is not the same process used for traditional advertising (the 30-second spots advertising Nike running shoes, Pop-Secret popcorn, or Pine Sol), where companies eye a particular hour—or even particular minute—and purchase that spot to promote their product. Infomercials are placed into either specifically dedicated time slots for half-hour infomercial programs or spread out more throughout the day for 2-minute spots.

Advice from the Pros

The key to buying media is buying media right.
—Ron Popeil

The space they buy may be on regional or local cable channels, network television—regional and national—or syndication. The space they seek out is broken down in "day parts" (for example, 6 a.m. to 10 a.m., 10 a.m. to 2 p.m.) and are spaces that the stations haven't yet sold, otherwise known as "remnant spaces." Each and every month stations have excess inventory, and they want to sell it. The costs of these spots can be as low as $90 or as much as $2,000. It depends on the reach of the station, the time of day, and other factors. The time is sold at a discount as compared to traditional advertising because of the fact that it is purchased on short notice based on what is readily available.

Advice from the Pros

An experienced direct response media agency will prove invaluable in ensuring that your product is running on the right media at the right price.
—Dick Weschler, president and CEO, Lockard & Weschler Direct, media buying agency

Ultimately, all of this detail, from when the commercial will run to whether it's running on ESPN or the Oxygen channel, isn't a great concern for you because you will be guided by an expert from the media buying agency that you hire, but a little knowledge under your belt can't hurt.

Even if you produced your own spot or show, media buying is not something you can do yourself. You must hire a professional agency. Even if you know someone who is a seller at a local station, it is not recommended to try this yourself. Again, let the professionals do what they do best. Let's understand the challenge that the media buying agency goes through: They look at your product and determine its appeal and market (and, believe me, they will have great understanding of this): Is it just for women, men and women, or parents specifically? What's the demographic, and what's the best way to reach that demographic? With that, they will ascertain the best test markets for your product, whether it's the Northeast or Southwest, cable or local, ESPN or Lifetime.

Because media buyers have a great familiarity with many product categories and have probably worked recently with a product within your category, they know what stations and what times have been working best and can direct you accordingly. However, you do want to make sure that they choose a good mix of stations and times in the beginning since your goal is to find as broad an audience as possible for your product, especially for your initial media test. From the results of the initial testing to a broad audience you will be able to see for yourself which stations are working for your product and which are not.

Once they have made their determinations, the test will be about a week long. Expect to spend $5,000 to $10,000 for the initial test for your two-minute, and up to $15,000 to $20,000 for the long form. (Again, these costs don't have to be borne by you. If you have licensed your product to a marketing company, they will be borne by your licensee.)

The amount of money you budget for your test will vary based on your offer as well. If you determine that you want to test two price points ($29.95 versus $39.95, or three payments of $29.95 versus one payment of $69.95), then make sure you still spend enough on each offer to get an accurate read, both as a comparison of price and as a standalone. The media buying agency will try to buy similar time on similar types of stations, or even the same station at similar times on different days. This will allow you to compare your price offers on equal footing. And do not always assume that the less expensive price will perform better. Sometimes the multiple pay, though it adds up to more money, will pull better than the lower single pay figure (three payments of $29.95 versus one payment of $69.95) simply due to perception of the price, as the viewer hears the lower $29.95 figure, which provides more accessibility then the $69.95 price point. On the other hand, a higher price will sometimes convey the appearance of better quality, while a lower price will convey lesser quality because the viewer thinks the price may be "too good to be true" ($14.99 versus $29.99 for skin-care product as an example). Thus, sometimes a price that's too low can cause hesitancy in the consumer to pick up the phone and call. And this is why we test various price structures.

The media test will show you if there is truly an interest in your product beyond the friends and family who are always happy to say how great it is. You will have a real opportunity to see if your product is needed, if it is understood, and if people want it and are picking up the phone and ordering.

MEASURE THE RESULTS

After the first week of your test, you will look at the results. The first thing to look at will be how much money you cleared. In other words, if you budgeted $10,000 for the week, how much of the money was the media buying company able to spend? Because they are buying remnant space and you and many other companies are competing to buy this inexpensive last-minute space, the media company is not always able to spend what you budget. The company will put its orders in, but it won't know how much it actually spent until after the week ends (referred to as *clearance* or *dollars cleared*). The media company will provide you with a media report or "performance and revenue report" (see sample report in Appendix F), which shows you the market or stations that were purchased, the dollars spent on each particular station, the number of orders, total revenue, dollars cleared, and three other very important statistics:

1. Cost per order (CPO)
2. Performance ratio
3. Average revenue per order

The CPO is how much it costs to get your orders. We'll keep it very simple for the sake of our discussion: If you cleared $5,000 in media spending your first week and received 250 orders, your CPO would be $20 ($5,000 divided by 250 orders = $20). Thus, it cost you $20 to get each order.

A good rule of thumb to keep in mind is that your CPO should be about the same level as the selling price of your product. That is, if you have a $20 selling price for your product and your CPO is $20, you're doing well in terms of response to your ad.

As another example, if you have cleared the same $5,000 in media spending and your total number of orders was only 100, your CPO would be $50 ($5,000 divided by 100 orders = $50 per order).

This would not be considered a good response based on your selling price. Conversely, if you multiply your CPO ($50) by your number of orders (100), you will get your net media spending ($5,000). I will explore overall costs and cost analysis toward the end of the chapter.

Another way of looking at your sales is the *performance ratio*, which equals the sales revenues divided by the net media spending. Before we go into the quantitative details, keep in mind that revenue includes the sales of your item, shipping and handling, and any up-sells in the offer (for example, "Buy two and receive an extra one free" or "Buy a deluxe version with an AC adapter and travel case"). Revenues change on a per-order basis due to the different possibilities offered. Some people will buy the up-sells while others will not. Some callers will ask for faster shipping, and they'll pay extra for that. Sometimes people order several quantities of your item. Thus, as an example, if on your 250 orders your total revenue is $10,000 and you have spent $5,000 on media, your performance ratio is 2:1 (the total revenue divided by your net media expenditure).

Our third factor is the average revenue per order. This number in its simplest definition indicates the average amount of revenue or sales achieved on a per-order basis. Thus, if you had 250 orders and your gross revenues were $10,000, your average revenue per order was $40 ($10,000 divided by 250 orders). This number is important as it tells you how well your overall program is going and how effective your telemarketing script is.

You are probably asking, "How are my revenues $40 per order if I am only selling a $20 product?" and "How am I making money if it costs me $20 to get each order (CPO = $20)? Well, let's get into that.

The way to do this is to work backward and first understand your costs as they relate to your revenues and then how the CPO relates to all of that.

Let's take a $19.99 item. Based on the cost structure previously described, you should have a cost of goods (COG) that is 1/5 to 1/6 of the selling price. Thus, the cost for your product should be between $3.30 and $4.00. Then you need to add in your other costs: freight, duty, royalties, telemarketing, credit card processing, and fulfillment (that is, shipping and handling). You will also have other costs that are hard to determine at this time such as returns and allowances, extra processing, and miscellaneous fees. On the revenue side you will have your product, shipping and handling, and product up-sells (additional products, warranties, deluxe kits, third-party up-sells, express shipping, and so on). Using this example and the simplest definitions of costs and revenues, allow me to illustrate:

Cost

Product COG	$3.50
Giveaway item (COG)	$1.25
Up-sell 1 (25% of $2.00 COG deluxe kit)	$0.50
Up-sell 2 (12% of $0.50) warranty up-sell)	$.06
Freight and duty (main products) (10%)	$0.47
Royalties 2% (producer/talent)	$0.40
Telemarketing (5 minutes per call at $0.90/min)	$4.50
Shipping and handling	$4.00
Total Cost	**$14.68**

Revenue

Product	$20.00	(19.95)
Up-sell 1 (35% buy on $9.95 deluxe up-sell)	$3.50	

Up-sell 2 (15% buy on $9.95 Warranty up-sell)	$1.50
Shipping and handling	
(with additional for up-sells)	$12.00
Priority Shipping*	$0.50
Total revenue	**$37.50**

(*Cost of priority shipping is $9.95, but only 5 percent of buyers take this option for this example.)

Thus, without your media spending, your gross profit would be $37.50 (gross revenue) less $14.68 (total cost), leaving you with the ability to spend $22.82 ($37.50−$14.68) on media. Therefore, if your CPO is $20 as above, you will leave yourself with a net profit of $2.82 per unit. Now that may not seem like a lot, but trust me, this is good. If you sell just 500 units per week, with your average revenue per order of $37.50, a CPO of $20, you are making $1,410 per week net on DR TV. And that's with spending only $10,000 per week. If you can hold those numbers at spending level of $50,000 per week, that's almost $7,000 earned per week.

Now, obviously there are some other costs involved in coordinating all of this, but these are the basics. They are presented in simple form to illustrate a potential scenario, based on those basics. The reality of the numbers will change as a result of your actual costs and responses, but the above can be used as a guideline to determine your program from your cost of product to your up-sells, and give you some insight on what to expect.

By hiring outside companies—such as telemarketing, fulfillment, and media buying—the operational aspect becomes relatively easy. Nevertheless, take your time in growing because you want to make sure you can manage your growth. Just as this illustrates how you can make money in what appears to be an easy manner, you can lose as well. As you increase what you spend on TV, your performance may drop off. You can have a bad week for a variety of reasons, from beautiful weather driving everyone away from their televisions and world news events forcing them to tune into major news channels where your shows are not running to running your infomercial on stations that simply do not "pull" for your product. If things turn, you can spend $10, $20, or $30,000 and average a CPO of $40 and thus lose on every order. For example: $37.50 (gross revenue) − $1,468 (total cost) = $22.82 (to spend on media), less $40.00 (CPO) = $16.10 (your loss per order).

The bottom line? Watching your media buying and performance on a daily basis is extremely important, and all good media agencies will help evaluate performance for you on a per-station-per-day basis. They will cut what does not work and add on to what does.

As a basic rule of thumb: If your product is being sold at a 5 to 6 multiple (5 to 6 times your cost of goods, or manufacturing cost), you want to achieve a minimum of a 2:1 performance ratio, or a CPO in the range of your item's selling price. Obviously, a lower CPO of, say, $15 or $10 would be phenomenal, especially in today's market where the cost of media, even for remnant, is high due to all the increased competition from corporations and new companies entering the wonderful world of DR.

In concert with the above information, you can also find out how well your telemarketing company is performing by looking at what is called the *conversion rate*. This is the number of people who call versus the number of orders taken. The higher the conversion from caller to customer, the better the company is doing. Average conversion rates are 55 to 60 percent (meaning, if 100 people call and 60 of them order your product, the call center is performing where they should be).

If you've got a conversion rate of 80 percent, your call center has done an exceptional job. Or more likely, you have done an exceptional job determining a need in the market and communicating your product's unique features to consumers, and the consumers have very few questions and apprehensions and just want to order your product. The opposite can happen as well. If your conversion rate is low, then most likely all of your numbers will be low (CPO and performance ratio), but this does not mean that you should give up on your product. In fact, this is where the work begins in the analysis stage. (A sample telemarketing report is included as Appendix G.)

Advice from the Pros

To keep conversion rates as high as possible, offer the call center employees a discount on your product as a thank-you gift from you. You can also send a quick 15-second sound bite via e-mail, especially to the work-at-home agents, thanking them for doing a great job taking your calls.

—Kimberly Fairfield-Frieders, director, sales, West Corporation, telemarketing company

To do a full analysis, you need to determine first if anyone called to place an order. Then find out if you received a good number of calls based on the dollars spent. If you converted at 60 percent, what would your results have been? Sometimes it is not the product as much as it is the message. Maybe people do need or want your product, but they really do not understand how it works. (See the Direct Response Marketing Success Story in Chapter 8 for an example of this situation.) If, however, your conversion is within the norm for the call center and your CPO is high and your performance ratio is low, say, $60 CPO and 0.9:1 ratio, you should probably call it a day on this product, at least through DR. You might instead try the grassroots to retail approach. Or you might go back to the drawing board and correct, modify, or reinvent. In other words, *don't* give up . . . *Keep moving.*

If you have success in the test phase, you, or the licensee, will move to the roll-out stage. This should be done slowly and methodically by expanding the amount of money spent on media marketing. Through the test, the media buyer will have learned what stations worked best for your item (for example, your item sold very well on

Oxygen, with a $10 CPO, but on the Sci-Fi Channel, your CPO was $120), and they will go after the space that was strongest, cutting out the stations that didn't perform. The company will purchase media as necessary, expanding as the item's success allows, spending as much as $500,000 per week in the short-form world.

One word of caution: Make sure you are all set with your production and manufacturing and timeliness of shipments. This is very important because when you take orders and charge credit cards, you must be able to ship. That is why I stress that if your product is successful, you want to roll out the increased marketing campaign slowly and methodically. Make sure all of your operations are in place—manufacturing, warehousing, fulfillment, telemarketing, and media buying. Also, after you have tested successfully, you can pull back for a little bit and take the time to get all of that in order. An item that is good this week should be good in two weeks as well, so don't worry. Get it all together, and do it right.

Over time your sales will trail off on the "exclusive TV offer," but this is not because interest in your product is waning. Instead, it is a mere fact of DR TV advertising, especially with short-form ($19.99) products over long-form products. In short form it is understood that 90 percent of the people who have seen and liked your product will not buy on TV; they will buy it only at retail stores. So the longer you are successful on TV without being at retail, the more the demand will build for your product. Thus, when you begin to offer your successful TV product to the retail marketplace, you are sure to be a success in that arena as well. As matter of fact, the retailers will be anxious to have your product as you have now more than proven market viability with your success.

In the world of long-form products, however, the ratios and numbers hold true to form and take on a different life as both the life cycle and the time to build to achieve results can vary greatly from the short-form format. In addition, you can achieve great success on TV by *not* making your product available at retail—"not available in stores." Again, this exclusivity works well in both formats, but because of the time you have with your viewer in long form, you can build that bond and build a following that provides you with the longer lifespan. There are many other facets to the long form and running a successful campaign, and this is why your partners in media, production, telemarketing, and so on are all very important. Again, they are the experts on the market; you are the expert on your product.

So, again, it is with this pent-up demand for your item by those who do not buy through television but are happy to do so at their local stores that will build your success. This is of course what you want for your product. And at this point, your DR TV commercials become a tool, with their endless impressions, to remind your customers that your product is out there and where they can find it.

It is then that your item becomes the next Edgemaster, Boogie Bass, Ab Roller, Showtime Rotisserie, Pasta Pro, Thigh-Master . . . the Next Big Thing. You'll have achieved what so many seek to do, and you did it because you had the patience, understanding, know-how, and, most importantly, the drive.

If you've got a great idea and you keep pushing for it to succeed, there is every possibility that your idea *will* succeed, and you will have achieved your MOST. As long as you keep believing in yourself and your product(s), and you believe that this business can work for you, *operators will be standing by!*

 ### Direct Response Marketing Success Story

The Low Conversion: Heavy Calls, Light Orders

I worked with one company to create a workout vest (described in Chapter 7) that would help consumers burn fat and build muscle while just walking around.

We developed the product, all the up-sells, and a great 2-minute spot. We set up budget for the first week, and we set up our first test.

(continued)

The results came in: dismal at best. The CPO was close to $100. Normally at that point, we would "punt." However, after looking at the telemarketing report, we realized the problem was not the lack of interest in the product. Actually, we had received a lot of calls. Apparently, the calls were taking 20 percent longer than the average 4.5 minutes, and the conversion rate was low, less than 15 percent. What did that tell us?

It told us one of two things: Either the operator at the telemarketing company was not clearly communicating for purposes of closing the sale, *or* the customer calling was very confused about something pertaining to the product itself.

Either way, one thing was clear: The item was of interest to the buying public, but we were not communicating our message clearly, either through our telemarketing or our DR spot itself.

How did we solve this? Well, we listened to a few calls, and we spoke with a few operators. It turned out the callers *were* drawn in by our claims of fat burning and the efficiency of the product, but they could not understand the functionality—our demonstration in our DR spot was not clear.

By leaving many questions unanswered in our commercial, we left the potential customers intrigued enough to call, but with too many questions, which built up their hesitancy in ordering the product.

Had we converted 60 percent of the calls we received, we would have achieved a CPO of closer to $38.00 on a $39.95 product. We would have been in hitting distance of a success.

We took some time to re-edit the commercial and our telemarketing script, and then we tried it all again. The conversion rates went up, now to 55 percent. However, ultimately, our CPO was still too high as the call volume was just not heavy enough. We could have gone in and tweaked again, but we felt the item had peaked. So we shipped a few and accepted the overall results as a short-term success, and we went on to work on the many other items we had waiting in the wings.

Lessons:

1. After you test your commercial, look at all the numbers because one number does not tell the whole story. A high CPO might occur for various reasons, and you should explore them.

(continued)

2. Always look at the CPO as it relates to your telemarketing conversion numbers. You might find you have a product that attracts many potential customers. The product is interesting enough for them to call, but your message is unclear.

3. Be prepared to test your commercial a few times, and be prepared to change, or edit, the original show because you will always view your show differently after you see the sales results.

4. Know when to cut your losses. If you tried a few price points, you have decent conversions on calls coming in, but you are still not pulling the numbers, then cut your losses and move on.

KEY CONCEPTS TO REMEMBER

1. Hire a media company familiar with your product category.

2. Hire a telemarketing company familiar with DR marketing.

3. Test and retest if necessary.

4. Understand all of your costs and all of the marketing aspects that affect revenue.

5. Analyze your results. Take the time to read them and understand them. The numbers don't lie.

6. Understand the effect of the cost of media on your CPO. Free media means each order costs you nothing, and the less you pay, the better off you are.

7. Understand how to read both your media report and your telemarketing report. Look at all the numbers, and then make an educated decision on what to do going forward.

8. Take your time. The right time to launch a product is when it's ready; the right time to roll out is when you are ready (based on your low CPO, of course).

9. Know when to quit. Cut your losses if it isn't working; don't fall in love with your product.

10. When it is working and you begin to roll out, move forward quickly, seize the moment, exploit the opportunity, and make lots of money. Enjoy!

In Closing

Infomercials and direct response marketing are ultimately all about risk and reward. Whether you're headed to the infomercial stage or your item is being sold to retail outlets, remember that you or the marketing company you work with takes on a huge financial risk. The consumers must buy it, use it, and not return it. That item must continue to sell and have at least a modicum of success for it to be worth the outlay of money and time. But, when they work, they work big, and the payoff is great!

To begin with, you should always focus on getting your product developed properly, and fully understand how it will need to be positioned into the marketplace for the consumer. Do your homework, and be as prepared as you can be for every stage of the process. And remember, if you are working with a DR marketing company, they are professionals and will know better than you, at least for now, how to proceed. But now that you armed with an education you'll be able to successfully work alongside them.

The more knowledge you have of this industry and the better understanding you have of its inner workings, the more prepared you will be in all of your negotiations at each stage. And if you do choose to raise your own money, you will be more prepared for the undertaking before you and for the bumps you may encounter along the way.

But while you should be wary of bumps, there is absolutely one thing you can count on in this business: There are enough professionals more than willing to work with you and help you as you head up this path. Like any industry, there are of course those you must watch out for, but sharks of this nature are few and far between in my experience. And at any time you want more participation or want to take on a partner, or just want some help and direction, it is always easily arranged.

Keep in mind one practical concept: Everyone wants to make money. That's why the professionals want to help you. From the telemarketing companies to the fulfillment to the media buyers and marketers, they will help. Maybe you're the next Ron Popeil, and maybe your concept is the Next Big Thing. Those you deal with will want success as much as you do. They'll meet you, see your invention, and understand that it's your MOST, and they'll commit some risk in hopes of sharing in the process and thus the reward with you.

When it all works well, that reward is great—for you and for them. So *keep moving* and remember:

Operators are standing by . . .

Appendix A

Licensing Your Product: Real-World Considerations in the Direct Response Marketplace

Whether you have gone through the direct response marketing process alone or with partners, and whether you have gotten a patent for your product or financing for your infomercial, it's important to consider an alternate way to market your product: licensing.

In the simplest of definitions, *licensing* is giving permission to a company to manufacture and sell your product.

The advantages of this option for your product have been discussed, and the purpose of this appendix is not to dissuade you from going the distance on your own or with your financial partners. Instead, it is merely meant to provide you with further information about the process and to ensure that whatever decision you do make is an educated one. To help you make the best possible decision for your product and your business, let's look more closely at how licensing works and the basic deal structure that goes with that choice. Ultimately, for your first product, it is *the* recommended way to go.

Keep in mind everything you have learned throughout this book as you negotiate with potential marketing companies. This knowledge will serve you well and also earn you possibly higher percentages because the companies you speak with will respect your understanding of the marketplace and ability to fill consumer needs, and thus will value you beyond the product you bring to the table.

Advice from the Pros

When looking to license your product, protect yourself. Don't take the first offer. Get several bids, and hear different strategies.

—Barbara Tulipane, president and CEO, Electronic Retailing Association

And you do have a lot of knowledge now. You know what is involved in the process of creating, developing, and bringing to market your product. You know the costs at each level, and more important, you know all the product-related expenses from going to market via the infomercial. So let's look further at the reality of what a DR marketing company has to pay for when it does its job, both the obvious and not-so-obvious costs. The DR marketing company will pay for the production of the infomercial (of course, if you have already produced one, this will be a plus as you negotiate your deal), and they will pay royalties to the producer and commissions to the sales reps who sell your item to the retailers (Wal-Mart, Walgreens, and others). They will also pay for getting your product into the country from the manufacturing plant. And they will pay for warehousing and providing the infrastructure for packaging, marketing, and distributing the product. They will assume the risks as mentioned above for inventory and excesses sold into retailers. And there's also product liability insurance—you never know when someone will contact the company saying he or she has been hurt, lost a finger, or blew up the kitchen due to your invention. All of those things are covered by the production company, and those burdens will not fall on your shoulders. These are extremely important aspects and should not be overlooked.

If you have licensed out your product to a DR marketing company, then, as mentioned, the investment in the infomercial, no matter how great or small, is not borne by you. Plus, if you have gone that far and paid for the infomercial production yourself, you can negotiate for reimbursement of costs as part of your upfront payment.

Under a licensing arrangement you will *not* be selling your item outright to a company. Sometimes the company will offer you an upfront fee, usually more of a "good-faith amount" toward the project—somewhere in the $5,000 to $10,000 range. The reason this good-faith amount is only sometimes given is that most DR marketing companies spend a lot of money bringing your product to market, and they often view that heavy investment in the legal aspects, production of the infomercial, and cost of buying the initial media as the upfront money.

The real payoff will be in the royalties you earn. The DR marketing company will create the infomercial and will sell your item, taking on all costs associated with the entire process. Some of these other costs also include product modifications, manufacturing costs, additional legal costs, packaging design, and other ancillary marketing costs—all of this in addition to the cost of production and the media costs. But you will earn royalties from the sales of your item. There are two ways you will likely earn them: First, you will earn royalties from *direct sales*—that is, those sales made via TV/Web/radio or print directly to the consumer. Second, you will earn royalties on *wholesale sales*—that is, the sales of your product made to any retailer (stores like Sears or Target), catalog companies, or even Internet sites, unless the marketing company has its own site, in which case you would be paid on the basis of a *direct-to-consumer sale*.

Royalties vary from 1 to 5 percent of the sale. A rule of thumb is that the percentage of royalties from your TV sales will be 50 percent of the amount you would receive from your retail sales. That is, your retail royalty will be *double* the royalty that you receive on TV (direct) sales. Why? It's simple math: On TV your item sells for, let us say, $30. But when your item sells for $30 at a retail shop like Amazon.com or Best Buy, those stores bought it for only $15. Ultimately, getting 2.5 percent of $30 (TV sales) and getting 5 percent of $15 (retail sales) will result in your making the same amount of money per item sold, no matter the venue.

Generally, what you will find is that the marketing companies that market products through long-form will offer you 2 percent on retail sales and 1 percent on TV sales. The marketing companies for short-form programs will usually pay 3 to 5 percent on retail and 1 to 3 percent on TV or direct-to-consumer sales. Also, it is important to understand with regard to the royalty arrangement that in the beginning a product can be profitable on TV, but inevitably, and soon after the launch, the TV sales can and will slow down, especially as the product becomes more available through retail outlets. It is because of this slow down in sales on TV that a marketing company might pay a disproportionately lower royalty on products sold from TV. It's not because they are unscrupulous; rather, it's because in order to continue driving sales and building demand at retail they need to continue to advertise, and the more they pay out in terms of costs, the less their ability to advertise on TV.

Understand that it is in the best interests of everyone to keep costs as low as possible when running a TV item because the greater the financial ability the company has to advertise, the more it will be able to drive sales at retail. Thus, the marketing company might even continue to run its TV campaign at a loss for the purpose of driving more business at retail because the sales volume potential at retail is far greater, as we have learned, and more profitable. This is an important fact to understand. The revenues generated from TV sales help fund more media, and the more media you can purchase, the more you will help drive sales at retail. Obviously, if a marketing company is following a pure "not available in stores" approach, they will only run their program on TV, on the Web, or through other direct-to-consumer venues. Thus, the above does not apply, so you will want to achieve as high a royalty as possible for direct-to-consumer sales because there is no retail portion.

Like anything else, these percentage rates are negotiable, and companies take other factors into consideration as well, including the uniqueness of product, strength of patent (broadness of claims and what is truly protected), proof of viability in the marketplace (track record of sales, no matter how limited), and manufacturing stage as presented (concept stage, prototype, or finished product).

Viability in the marketplace means that if you can show your particular product category is strong and that the risk of sell-though is mitigated, you stand to earn a higher percentage. For example, being first to market is great, but if it's a truly new market then there's no proven market viability, and as such you lose some leverage in initial negotiations. However, if you create an exercise item and your item is, for example, another abdominal exercise device . . . well, it's been proven that "ab" devices sell far better than, say, triceps devices, and thus you already have proven market viability, from a category perspective, and you have a little more strength at the bargaining table.

Last, manufacturing is an important aspect. Has a factory actually produced your product yet? Has it created a tool or mold for your product? Have the bugs in the manufacturing process been discovered and corrected? Do you even have a manufacturer? Don't worry if your answer is "no" to these questions—it is okay. But they should be kept in mind when negotiating, because the more you have accomplished and the more questions you can answer, the more leverage you have and thus the higher the royalty will most likely be.

All in all, the further you are along in the process, the more leverage you have in your negotiations. And, yes, it is possible to go beyond the 5 percent. If, for instance, you have already successfully sold your product on QVC or tested your commercial yourself and achieved a low CPO, you've proven consumer demand and viability in the marketplace. This allows you to have more input and, as mentioned, get into the higher percentage brackets—or even get a profit-sharing arrangement.

I have had many inventors ask me, "Why shouldn't I get 50 percent of the profits? Why should I only get 3 or 1 percent of sales when, without *my* product, they would have nothing?" The answer is simple: It all comes down to financial risk and understanding the marketplace. Yes, you risked a lot of your time and money to get to the point of licensing your product, but bringing it to the next level involves a lot of risk—at least 10 times what you've already paid. And, even if your product is successful, there is still a continued cost and great risk. Because you never (I repeat, never!) know when sales will just end, possibly leaving you with a lot of product in inventory, or worse, on the shelves of retailers just waiting to be marked down in price and have that difference in profit charged back to the company that sold it to them.

The best way to make the least amount of money is to push and be greedy. Try to get what's fair, but don't let the green-eyed monster take hold of you. When negotiating, the DR marketing company will tell you they do not always make a great deal of money from the TV spots. This happens to be true. A product's success will really be found at retail, and if it performs well on TV, the DR marketing company will be willing to stick with your product until the real financial gains can be found as your product becomes available at retail outlets around the country.

The point here is, do not be overly concerned with your TV royalty. Sure, you want that money, but the quick buck is not where the money is.

I want to be clear on this point. There is a great deal of money that *can* be made from TV sales when you have a successful product. Products featured in long form sometimes never even go the retail route ("not available in stores"). These shows can be very lucrative, and your product can have a relatively long lifespan. In short form (two-minute spots), the experience is much different. You can achieve great success early on and make a lot of money—that is how you know you have a great product that will enjoy great success at retail. But the short-form success only lasts so long. In order to drive sales once at retail, you need to keep the spots running, even if they are not making as much, just to drive business through broadcasting constant TV impressions.

Studies that show only about 8 to 10 percent of viewers will ever buy a product via TV. No matter how great the product appears, they will not buy it until they can see, touch, and feel your product at a store they know and trust. So by heavily advertising, you are actually building a demand for your product. You *will* want your product to be available at retail stores because, again, if it's a hit on TV, you'll do 10 times that amount through the retail channel.

When negotiating royalties, keep all of this in mind. One approach I recommend is starting with a particular royalty while the product is advertised on TV and *not* yet available at retail. Then, once the product is made available at retail, reduce the royalty for the TV portion. By suggesting this in your negotiations, you will show your understanding of the business and your willingness to be flexible and create a win-win for everyone involved. Let's take a step back for a moment and focus on only the short-form arena. There are marketing companies that will want to market your product on your behalf, but they will charge *you*. As stated earlier in the book, when you encounter this, tread carefully. They charge about $25,000 to $50,000 to produce a two-minute spot and more to test your product ("testing" meaning the commercial will air on TV). These companies will make certain promises about the amount of testing they will do and the treatment of your product. Again, be wary. As in any area where the uninitiated get an opportunity like this for a leg up, there are companies that are just not "above board." Such companies have been known to provide reports that do not accurately reflect what media they purchased, and they make it hard to ascertain if that report is even for your product. Though you should *not* go the route of paying a company to market your product, if for some reason you choose to do so, you will want a lawyer to look over the contracts, check references from the company to see what other products they have handled, and check with authorities such as the Better Business Bureau (BBB.org) to see if any complaints have been lodged against them.

In conclusion, if you decide to license your product, you should definitely negotiate the best deal you can get. But you must remember there are many more inventors than there are DR marketing companies, and believe it or not, there are many very good products. Ultimately, the inventor is more expendable than you might think. Your item may be great, but someone else will have a great item too. All of this is important to consider at the negotiating table. Again, your goal on your first item is to *make the deal!* Prove your inventions can create wealth, that you know how to fill a need, you have great ideas, and you are easy to work with. Make yourself wanted, and next time, *you* will be sitting in the driver's seat because you have a proven success and a good track record. And, you have found your MOST.

Appendix B

Sample Patent Attorney's Retainer Agreement

TODAY'S DATE:
Via E-Mail
NAME:
ADDRESS:

Re: Retention of Legal Services

Dear (Name):

We are pleased that you wish to retain our firm to represent you in intellectual property matters.

Conflicts

We are unaware of any conflict with regard to the particular matters for which you have requested our aid. If, however, during the course of our firm's representation of your company, we become aware of potential conflicts of interest, we will immediately inform you of such.

(continued)

Duties of (Law Firm) and Client

We will provide legal services as necessary to represent you within the scope of this engagement. We shall keep you informed of our activities on your behalf and the status of your matters. When requested, we will provide you with an estimate of the fees and expenses for any proposed activity. Any estimate provided as to the cost of taking any action is simply an estimate and not binding unless we undertake such service on a flat-fee basis. You, in turn, shall keep us fully informed of all relevant facts with regard to any of your matters within the scope of our engagement, cooperate with us in pursuing your matter, pay our invoices for disbursements within 30 days, and keep us informed of your current address and telephone number.

Charges

Each attorney of the firm maintains a daily diary of client work performed and reasonable value for time expended in connection with the rendering of legal services. Each attorney has an hourly billing rate based on that attorney's experience and expertise, which is typically adjusted annually. The reasonable value for services rendered is generally the logged hours at the current billing rate of the individual attorneys. Certain types of services rendered by the firm may be billed at a flat fee rather than at an hourly billing fee rate. Most commonly, services involving preparation and filing of U.S. trademark applications, foreign patent and trademark applications, trademark renewals, patent and trademark assignments, and similar items may fall within this minimum-fee category. (LAW FIRM) will charge the client for charges and expenses incurred in rendering its services, including but not limited to telephone charges, photocopying, postage, filing fees, travel, and other necessary expenses.

(*continued*)

Trademarks

Searches: Before adopting, using, and attempting to register a trademark, it is advisable to make a search of the federal and state trademark registrations as well as common law rights in unregistered trademarks and trade names to determine if there are any prior conflicting rights. However, it should be noted that even the broadest search cannot guarantee that there would not be a conflict, particularly in those instances in which others have common law rights that have not been registered. The cost of such search is approximately $1,100, including fees and disbursements, if the search is conducted in the normal turnaround period of 7 to 10 days, with higher charges for searches conducted on an accelerated basis. A review of this report and our firm's opinion as to availability for use and registration are billed at the normal hourly basis. On average, such review takes approximately 1 to 2 hours. Due to the cost of a full search, particularly where either rapid turnaround is needed or a number of potential marks are to be reviewed for adaptation, we can perform a preliminary inhouse search of the federal and state registers for approximately $200, plus $50 disbursements for usage of the related online computer databases. The inhouse searches are not useful to make a final decision on a selected mark, but they can be used to eliminate marks where a near duplicate has previously been registered.

The above costs for searches are for a word mark. If the mark is a device or incorporates a design feature, the device must be separately searched. The device itself would have to be reviewed before advising as to the search requirements and costs.

Registration Costs: If the mark is in use in interstate commerce, application can be made for a federal registration, which offers numerous advantages and lays the basis for

(continued)

nationwide protection. If there is only an intention to use the mark in interstate commerce, an application could be made based on such intention, but a registration will not issue until the mark is in commercial use within the statutory period of three (3) years from the notice of allowance.

Our charges for trademark applications are assessed on a flat-fee basis. We charge $*XXX* to prepare and file a federal trademark application plus official filing fees of $325 for each class of goods or services. If the mark involves a design or lettering in a special format, there may be additional charges for preparation of appropriate drawings. If the application is based on intention to use, it will be necessary, at some time in the future to file a Statement of Use. If use does not occur within six months of the notice of allowance of the application, one or more extensions need to be filed with attendant costs. If the application is objected to or rejected by the examining attorney, additional costs will be incurred in connection with perfecting the application and obtaining the allowance. Such costs are incurred at the normal hourly rates.

In general, trademarks are protected on a territorial basis, that is, country by country. They must be cleared and registered under the laws of each country. We have local agents in all countries who assist us in protecting our clients' marks. In addition, if you have a bona fide place of business in one of the countries that are a party to the Madrid Protocol, we may be able to obtain an International Registration. There is now a Community Trademark which provides "supra-national" protection in the 15 countries of the European Community. If you are interested in filing in any particular country, we will be glad to provide specific information as to search, registration costs, and filing strategy.

(*continued*)

Patents

There are two types of patents: *Utility patents* are concerned with useful articles and methods, and *design patents* are directed to the appearance of goods. For an invention to be worthy of a patent, it must be unobvious over the state of the art at the time of its invention. In order to ascertain whether such is the case, we normally conduct a patent search to review the most relevant prior art. The results of such searches are then reviewed to ascertain the likelihood of success and, to a more limited extent, whether your invention is dominated by a prior patent. Searches usually do not uncover all possible relevant patents, and they should not be considered a full infringement search. Rather, they are to be used as a general aid to ascertain the current state of patenting on your system. Currently, searches vary between $700 and $1,000 depending on the nature of the invention and our analysis of the prior art. Our opinion letter normally takes between 1 and 2 hours of attorney time.

As can be seen from the accompanying price list, utility patent applications are not normally done on a flat-fee basis since the amount of services involved would depend on the subject matter. There are, however, a number of fixed costs in connection with the preparation of the application and its later prosecution. As a general rule of thumb, a relatively simple utility application would cost approximately $5,000 to $10,000, which would include all government fees, drawings, and other disbursements necessary for the filing. During prosecution, there most likely will be at least one Office Action requiring a response, and there will be issue fees of $700 (small entity) and publication fees of $300.

(*continued*)

Design patent applications are charged on a flat-fee basis ($*XXX*) for preparation and filing. Additional costs would include drawings at $125 to $150 a page and government fees of $215 (small entity). Depending on the number of drawings and the complexity of the invention, the costs can vary substantially. Prosecution of a design patent application usually includes responding to Office Actions on an hourly basis and, finally, issue fee payment of $400 (small entity) plus our flat fee of $*XXX* for this service.

Copyright

Software coding and screen images are protectable by copyright. Our charges are $ *XXX* including a $30 government fee. If we must respond to a Copyright Office's refusal to register, additional charges are assessed on an hourly basis.

Deposits

We require an advance of $_____. If this advance is exhausted, we may request additional deposits as needed. This advance should be replenished within ten (10) working days of our request. Client agrees that we have the right to require prepayment of out-of-pocket expenses, such as filing fees, before incurring such expenses.

Invoices

You will be invoiced monthly for the services rendered during the previous month. Occasionally, a monthly invoice may include charges or expenses from one or more preceding months that were not previously billed. Our invoices are due and payable when rendered. If an account is unpaid for more than thirty (30) days from the date of the invoice, it is considered overdue. We, at our discretion, may cease to undertake

(continued)

services until all overdue amounts are paid. There is a late charge for all invoices that have not been paid in full within sixty (60) days from the date of the invoice of 1 percent a month on the unpaid balance.

In the event of a fee dispute, we have been advised that our right to arbitration is in conformity with Part 1215 to Title 22 of the Official Compilations of Codes, Rules, and Regulations of the State of New York, effective March 4, 2002. Said arbitration is to take place before a single arbitrator in New York County, New York, with the prevailing party being entitled to recover its reasonable legal fees and the costs of said arbitration.

Withdrawal from Representation

We may withdraw our representation either with your consent or for good cause. Good cause includes nonpayment of disbursements and expenses, your refusal to cooperate with us, or any fact or circumstance that would render our continuing representation unlawful or unethical.

Disclaimer

We make no promises or guarantees about the outcome of any matter. Any comments concerning possible outcomes are merely opinion, and as such, they express no more than a possibility as to the outcome.

Lien

You grant us a lien on any and all claims or causes of action relating to legal representation of you by us. The lien will be for any money due us and will attach to any recovery you may obtain, whether by arbitration award, judgment, settlement, or otherwise.

(continued)

Complete Agreement

This written agreement contains all the terms and conditions of the agreement between you and us. There are no other terms or conditions. It may be modified only in writing as signed both by you and us.

Would you please acknowledge your receipt of this letter and acceptance of its terms by signing a copy of this letter at the place indicated below and returning it to us along with the retainer fee.

Very truly yours,

Our reference: (LAW FIRM)

The terms of this letter have been accepted by the undersigned this

_____ day of _____ 2006

Company

By

    Principal

Appendix C

Sample Short-Form Infomercial Script

TITLE: Smart Tape
SUBTITLE: Two Minutes

VIDEO	AUDIO
1. Talent walks into frame full shot.	Hi Folks. I'm Beau Rials, and this is Smart Tape, and there is absolutely nothing like it.
2. CU of Smart Tape in his hand.	This revolutionary digital tape measure will never let you forget or misread a measurement ever again.
3. Talent starts to measure a box that is in front of him.	Look how easy it is to use.
4. CU of the measure working.	Just take the measurement you want, read the exact figure on the digital display, and record the measurement.

(continued)

TITLE: Smart Tape *(continued)*	
VIDEO	AUDIO
5. ECU of the digital readout. (The numbers change.)	*One foot 2 and 3/8th inches (talent voice).*
6. CU of Beau (and records up to 20 seconds) on screen.	And now Smart Tape will remember that measurement for as long as you want.
7. *ECU of the digital readout. (The numbers change.)*	*One foot 2 and 3/8th inches (recorder voice).*
8. *CU of* Smart Tape, *pictures of cloth tapes, metal tapes, pens, pencils, scrap paper, and recording devices.*	Smart Tape makes ordinary tape measures obsolete.
9. Beau measures a cabinet.	The secret is the easy-to-read digital display and built-in voice recorder, which make forgetting or misreading measurements a thing of the past!
10. *CU of* Smart Tape.	This is a professional-strength digital tape measure that allows you to record your measurements as you take them.
11. CU of a pencil nib breaking (B roll).	So no more fumbling with pencils that break.
12. Pad with lots of numbers on it on; a very messy workbench (B roll).	No more losing that scrap of paper you scribbled on.

(continued)

TITLE: Smart Tape (*continued*)	
VIDEO	AUDIO
13. *Man on top of ladder; he can't find his pen, and he's trying to hold a piece of paper* (B roll).	This will never happen to you again.
14. *Same man on ladder takes measurement and records it directly into the tape measure.*	Now taking and remembering measurements is easy: Just take it . . . and tell it!
15. *ECU of the digital readout.*	***Pipe length 1 foot 2 1/2 inches (man's voice).***
16. Woman measures a curtain drop (B roll).	Use Smart Tape around the home (measure for shelves, carpet, a space for the TV, or even hanging pictures).
17. Woman in a fabric store.	And then retrieve your measurements when you need them.
18. *ECU of the digital readout.*	***Draperies 6 feet 3 inches (recorder voice).***
19. Measuring space under counter for dishwasher.	
20. Beau measuring a picture frame.	Smart Tape is perfect for your all your craft projects.
21. WS: Young girl finishes taking measurement.	It's so easy that anyone can use it! **Twelve inches (young girl's voice).**

(*continued*)

TITLE: Smart Tape (*continued*)

VIDEO	AUDIO
22. Beau using the Smart Tape to hang a picture.	And now you can hang pictures with precise accuracy, thanks to Smart Tape.
23. CU of magazine. CUT TO 24. Product shot.	To get the features of this cutting-edge technology, you would have to buy several items and spend over $60 (SEE ALTERNATE), but now thanks to this special TV offer, the Smart Tape can be yours for just $19.95!
25. Product shot.	But folks, there's still more: Call right now, and you'll get this amazing emergency self-powered flashlight—no batteries, no electricity—just light when you need it the most. A $20 value, yours free, when you order! That means you'll get it all: the revolutionary Smart Tape and the Amazing Smart Flashlight. An incredible $80 value for just $19.95. Here's how to order.
26. Product shot. (ALTERNATE)	

Appendix D

Sample Call to Action (CTA)

X Razor:
CTA Script 1 × $9.95—3 Years of Free Blades

SC	VIDEO	AUDIO
1.	Montage of sketches and blueprints of the X Razor. Use slow dissolves and drifts to cover . . . dissolve to . . .	It took 8 years of research and development . . . 60 worldwide patents in 20 countries. It's the closest, most comfortable shave you'll ever experience. And we guarantee it!
2.	Slow tilt-up of the X Razor as it revolves on a turntable. X Razor logo appears in the left corner.	This is the X Razor from (Company): The first and only triple-blade razor with patented multi-angle technology.

(continued)

X Razor: (*continued*)		
SC	VIDEO	AUDIO
	Super: ° Multiangle technology ° Triple blade	Traditional razors shave diagonally down the whisker, but the X Razor's unique multiangle technology allows each blade in succession to cut the whisker at the optimum shaving angle. The result is a truly close shave that leaves skin incredibly smooth.
3.	B-roll montage: CU of hot towels and straight-razor shaving process.	Professional barbers train for years to perfect their skilled technique of shaving with one blade at the optimum angle. It takes time . . .
4.	**Super:** ° $	**And** as a customer, **you** pay for it.
5.	MS model using X Razor. CU of model using X Razor.	Now, thanks to this amazing innovation in design and technology, you can achieve an even closer shave, with 3 perfectly angled balanced blades.
6.		And all in your own home . . . without the expensive price tag.
7.	Animation—Safety. Bad guy razor shot: Model nicking himself on a blade.	And the X Razor's patented safety guards keep the skin taut and lift the whisker for a truly close, comfortable shave with virtually no nicks, cuts, or irritations.

(*continued*)

X Razor: (*continued*)		
SC	VIDEO	AUDIO
8.		**Testimonials.**
9.	Model shaving against the grain.	You can even shave against the grain of your beard. Imagine doing this with your old razor . . .
10.	Model shaving. **Super:** ° 60 patents	With over 60 patents worldwide, this new multiangle technology is so superior . . .
11.	Dissolve to same model touching his face and smiling as a female model comes in from behind to rub her cheek against his.	It will amaze **you** . . . **And we guarantee it!**
12.	CU of quick-change X Razors. Longer-lasting animated GRX indicating that our blade lasts 30 to 50 percent longer.	Look how easy it is to change the blades.
13.	Model using the X Razor.	But we know that the only way that you can truly appreciate the X Razor's multiangle difference is to try it yourself. That's why we've created an offer you're just not going to believe.
14.	Product shot. 90-day guarantee.	The revolutionary X Razor Shaving System is yours to try—Risk Free—in your own home—for 90 days. That's 3 whole months—and your satisfaction is guaranteed! If for whatever reason you are not 100 percent satisfied, send

(*continued*)

X Razor: (*continued*)		
SC	**VIDEO**	**AUDIO**
	Super: ° 3 months	the X Razor back to us for a complete refund of the purchase price.
15.	Product shot. Price point build-up. ***Phone number banner is displayed up to the end.	You get the X Razor Shaving System—including the revolutionary X Razor—its stylish travel case and the 12 replacement cartridges valued at over $60!
16.	Product shot: 8 Lady X Razors. Product usage shot: Model using the Lady X Razor on her legs, touching and smiling.	Plus . . . At no additional cost to you: 8 of our ladies' multiuse disposables. Engineered with the same patented multiangle technology. This X Razor is designed specifically for a woman, leaving legs more silky, smooth, and irresistible! That's another $20 value!
17.	Montage of X Razors. CU dissolves through variety of tilts, pans, and zooms. **Super:** ° $240 value plus shipping and handling	But we've saved the best for the very last: If you call right now, we'll sign you up for this exclusive TV offer: 2 years of free replacement blades. Yes, you heard correctly. That's 128 replacement blades over 2 years delivered right to

(continued)

X Razor: (*continued*)		
SC	VIDEO	AUDIO
	Free! (Plus shipping and handling.)	your door, for free! All you have to do is pay the shipping and handling.
18.	Complete product shot . (pop on) **Super:** ° 90-day guarantee ° $9.95	In total, this entire offer including the X Razor, the deluxe travel case, 12 replacement cartridges, and 8 multiuse disposable X Razors—plus the 2 years of free blades and our incredible 90-day satisfaction guarantee is all yours for just one single payment of $9.95. That's right: Just one single payment of 9 dollars and 95 cents. How can we do this? It's very simple: We truly believe that once you try the X razor and discover that with it, your shaving experience is so much better than anything you've ever had, you will never use any other blade again!
19.	Model shaving.	Think about the money you already spend on shaving, and you'll see just how amazing this offer really is! Imagine the convenience of replacement blades' being shipped right to your door. But, wait: We're about to make this offer impossible to resist!

(*continued*)

X Razor: (*continued*)

SC	VIDEO	AUDIO
		Call now, and you'll get—as a special bonus—another entire year of **free** blades. That's right. You'll get not 1, not 2, but 3 years of free blades delivered right to your door. That's another year of replacement blades yours free. All you have to do is pay the shipping and handling! You do the math! That's hundreds of dollars in value all for just 1 single payment of $9.95. We believe in the X Razor so much and we're so sure you will be satisfied with it that you will become a customer for life!
20.		How can you afford not to call? Operators are standing by, and this limited offer will end. Call Now! And don't forget to ask our X Razor sales representative how you can get the ultimate in shaving luxury with the X Razor Royal Kit—specially priced when you call now!

Appendix E

Sample Telemarketing Scripts

INFORMATION BOX

$19.95 + $5.99 shipping and handling = $25.94.
New York and California residents, please add sales tax.

Smart Tape is an easy-to-use tape measure. An LCD screen clearly displays measurements as you take them, and it also includes a digital voice recorder that records up to 20 seconds. It easily switches between inches and centimeters. It includes batteries, handy wrist strap, and convenient belt clip. **Bonus**: Smart Light Flashlight—no batteries, no electricity, just squeeze the handle for light.

Up-sell:

1. Additional Smart Tape and Smart Light, $14.95 + $5.99 shipping and handling.

2. Lifetime replacement warranty, $4.99.

30-day money back guarantee.
Delivery: within 4 weeks.

ORDER SCRIPT

Smart Tape Measure

START RECORDING CALL HERE.

Zip code: _____

"To ensure proper handling, this call may be recorded."
(No restrictions for this statement. Trips all calls.)
If PR:
>   "May I continue?" _ (Y, N) (PRESS <PF10>)

If No:
>   "I'm sorry. I will not be able to process your request."
>   "Thank you for calling."
>   (PRESS <PF3> TO LOG AS AN INQUIRY.)

First name: _____ Last name: _____

"Which credit card would you prefer to use?" _ (M, V, A,
    S = Novus/Discover)
Card number: _____ Exp date: ____
(PRESS <PF7> TO VERIFY CREDIT CARD NUMBER.)

Address: _____
Apartment number: _____
City: _____ State: __

"May I have your e-mail address?" _ (Y, N) (PRESS <PF10>)
If Yes:
>   E-mail address: _____ ***IS: 40-byte field***
>   (FOLLOW THIS PATTERN: client@server.xxx)
>   (@ is shift 2) (NO SPACES)(ALWAYS VERIFY SPELLING.)

"As part of a special promotion, you may purchase an additional
Smart Tape for just $14.95 plus $5.99 shipping and handling billed
to the same account you are using today. May I add the additional
Smart Tape with the Smart Light bonus to your order?" _ (Y, N)

"Also, for a limited time only, you can receive a lifetime replacement warranty for only $4.99 billed to the same account you are using today." (If the caller has questions about the warranty, enter X here ___ ***IS: If X is entered, please supply/insert the following:*** "If for any reason your Smart Tape fails to work while you own it, just return it, and we'll replace it free of charge. You just pay the shipping and handling. May I add our lifetime warranty to your order?"

"The order will ship within 4 weeks. Thank you for calling."

STOP RECORDING CALL HERE.

CUSTOMER SERVICE SCRIPT

Smart Tape

START RECORDING CALL HERE.

NATURE OF CONCERN: _ (ENTER SELECTION AND PRESS <PF10>)

1. PRODUCT INFORMATION.

2. CHECK OR MONEY ORDER ADDRESS.

3. STATUS OF ORDER.

4. BILLING QUESTIONS.

5. RETURNS, CANCELLATIONS, OR REFUNDS.

If 1, 3, 4, 5:
    FOR CUSTOMER SERVICE, REFER CALLER TO:
      Smart Tape
      PO Box 5555
      Van Nuys, CA 91000-0000

    AND OFFER
    E-MAIL ADDRESS, ENTER X: _ (PRESS <PF10>)

If X:

"Please e-mail us at PRODUCTS at PRODUCT STRATEGIES INC dot COM (products@productstrategiesinc.com). Your e-mail will be answered within 24 hours."

If 2:

FOR CHECK OR MONEY ORDER, REFER CALLER TO:
SMART TAPE
~~ Check or money order address ~~

"Please make your check in the amount of $25.94, which is $19.95 plus $5.99 shipping and handling."

<u>STOP RECORDING CALL HERE.</u>

"Thank you for calling."
PRESS "ENTER" TO LOG CUSTOMER SERVICE CALL.

DOCUMENTED INQUIRY SCRIPT

_ ENTER SELECTION. (PRESS <ENTER> TO LOG CALL.)
1 = PRICING OR PAYMENT PLAN QUESTION.
2 = PRODUCT INFORMATION. CALLER REQUESTED
    INFORMATION.
3 = CALLER INTERRUPTED. WILL CALL BACK.
4 = MISUNDERSTOOD OFFER. REFUSED TO ORDER.
5 = GHOST OR PRANK CALL.
6 = OTHER.

KEY

<u>Bold Underlined Text:</u> Represents instructions to IS.
CAPITALIZED TEXT: Represents instructions to the telerepre-
                    sentative.

Appendix F

Sample Media and Telemarketing Reports

TELESERVICES CORPORATION

E-MAIL TRANSMITTAL:

DATE: 01/16/2004   ORDER DATE(S): 1/15/04

TO: MICHAEL PLANIT
    PRODUCT STRATEGIES

E-MAIL ADDRESS: MICHAEL@PRODUCTSTRATEGIESINC.COM
SHEET NO: 01

FROM: TELESERVICES CORPORATION

RE: SOURCE REPORTS

CLIENT   PRODUCT

403200   STIKI

          * DENOTES PRODUCTS WITH ZERO COUNTS

REPORTS INCLUDED:
     SOURCE COUNT REPORT(S)
     SOURCE HOUR I REPORT(S)
     Daily Count By Hour Report(s)

RESTRICTIONS: Send only cover sheet if zero counts

NO. OF PAGES: 4

CLIENT NUMBER: 403200
PRODUCT ID : STIKI   PRODUCT DESCRIPTION - STIKIBOARD

SOURCE CODE	STATE	SOURCE TYPE	NUMBER DIALED	ORDER CALLS	REFERRAL CALLS	INQUIRY CALLS	DOC C/S CALLS
FAMILY NET		CABLE	800-417-9595	4	0	0	0
WB NETWORK		CABLE	800-413-1818	3	0	0	1

** SOURCE TOTALS **   7   0   0   1

** PRODUCT TOTALS **

TOTAL CALLS	8	U.S. - 8	CANADA - 0
TOTAL ORDER CALLS	7	U.S. - 7	CANADA - 0
TOTAL REFERRAL CALLS	0	U.S. - 0	CANADA - 0
TOTAL INQUIRY CALLS	0	U.S. - 0	CANADA - 0
TOTAL DOC C/S CALLS	1	U.S. - 1	CANADA - 0
TOTAL UPSELL YES	2	U.S. - 2	CANADA - 0
TOTAL UPSELL QUANTITY	1	U.S. - 1	CANADA - 0
TOTAL UPSELL ONE	0	U.S. - 0	CANADA - 0
TOTAL REBUTTAL REBUY	0	U.S. - 0	CANADA - 0
TOTAL UPSELL TWO YES	0	U.S. - 0	CANADA - 0
TOTAL ORDER CALLTIME	2,016	U.S. - 2,016	CANADA - 0
TOTAL INFO ONL CALLTIME	0	U.S. - 0	CANADA - 0
TOTAL REFERRAL CALLTIME	0	U.S. - 0	CANADA - 0
TOTAL INQUIRY CALLTIME	0	U.S. - 0	CANADA - 0
TOTAL DOC C/S CALLTIME	248	U.S. - 248	CANADA - 0
TOTAL TOTAL CALLTIME	2,264	U.S. - 2,264	CANADA - 0
TOTAL CA TAX	7	U.S. - 7	CANADA - 0
TOTAL CREDIT CARD	0	U.S. - 0	CANADA - 0
TOTAL NY TAX	7	U.S. - 7	CANADA - 0
TOTAL REBUT INQ	7	U.S. - 7	CANADA - 0
TOTAL UPSELL 2 UPSELL 2	8	U.S. - 8	CANADA - 0
TOTAL ANI CAPTURE	0	U.S. - 0	CANADA - 0
TOTAL #1 ON C/ SCREEN	1	U.S. - 1	CANADA - 0
TOTAL C/S 2 C/S 2	0	U.S. - 0	CANADA - 0
TOTAL C/S 3	0	U.S. - 0	CANADA - 0
TOTAL C/S #4 P/BILL	0	U.S. - 0	CANADA - 0
TOTAL C/S 5	0	U.S. - 0	CANADA - 0
TOTAL DOC INQ 1	0	U.S. - 0	CANADA - 0
TOTAL DOC INQ 2	0	U.S. - 0	CANADA - 0
TOTAL DOC INQ 3	0	U.S. - 0	CANADA - 0
TOTAL DOC INQ 4	0	U.S. - 0	CANADA - 0
TOTAL DOC INQ 5	0	U.S. - 0	CANADA - 0
TOTAL DOC INQ 6	0	U.S. - 0	CANADA - 0
TOTAL UPSLL QUANTIT	7	U.S. - 7	CANADA - 0
TOTAL UPSLL NO UPSLL NO	5	U.S. - 5	CANADA - 0

The following sources did not generate any calls:

BIO   COURT   LIFE-MOVIE   OXYGEN   SOAPNET

END OF PRODUCT

ICSC6010 Ver. 01

CLIENT NUMBER -403200
PRODUCT ID - STIKI   PRODUCT DESCRIPTION - STIKIBOARD

SOURCE CODE --- HOURS ---

	0000	0100	0200	C300	0400	0500	0600	0700	0800	0900	1000	1100	1200	1300	1400	1500	1600	1700	1800	1900	2000	2100	2200	23C
FAMILY NET 800-417-9595																								
ORD CNT	0	0	0	0	0	0	0	0	0	0	0	0	0	0	0	1	0	0	0	0	0	0	0	0
REF CNT	0	0	0	0	0	0	0	0	0	0	0	0	0	0	0	0	0	0	0	0	0	0	0	0
INQ CNT	0	0	0	0	0	0	0	0	0	0	0	0	0	0	0	0	0	0	0	0	0	0	0	0
DCS CNT	0	0	0	0	0	0	0	0	0	0	0	0	0	0	0	0	0	0	0	0	0	0	0	0
WB NETWORK 800-413-1818																								
ORD CNT	0	0	0	0	0	0	0	1	1	0	0	1	0	0	0	0	0	0	0	0	2	0	0	0
REF CNT	0	0	0	0	0	0	0	0	0	0	0	0	0	0	0	0	0	0	0	0	0	0	0	0
INQ CNT	0	0	0	0	0	0	0	0	1	0	0	0	0	0	0	0	0	0	0	0	0	0	0	0
DCS CNT	0	0	0	0	0	0	0	1	0	0	0	0	0	0	0	0	0	0	0	0	0	0	0	0
TOTALS:																								
ORD CNT	0	0	0	0	0	0	0	1	1	0	0	1	0	1	0	1	0	0	0	0	2	0	0	0
REF CNT	0	0	0	0	0	0	0	0	0	0	0	0	0	0	0	0	0	0	0	0	0	0	0	0
INQ CNT	0	0	0	0	0	0	0	0	1	0	0	1	0	1	0	0	0	0	0	0	0	0	0	0
DCS CNT	0	0	0	0	0	0	0	1	0	0	0	0	0	0	0	0	0	0	0	0	0	0	0	0

COUNTER TOTALS FOR PRODUCT: STIKI

		U.S.		CANADA
TOTAL CALLS	-	8	-	-
ORDER-COUNT	-	7	-	-
REFERRAL-COUNT	-	0	-	-
INQUIRY-COUNT	-	0	-	-
DOC-CS-COUNT	-	1	-	-
UPSELL-YES	-	2	-	-
UPSELL-QTY	-	1	-	-
REBUTTAL-1-YES	-	0	-	-
REBUTTAL-QTY	-	0	-	-
UPSELL-2-YES	-	0	-	-
ORDR-CALLTIME	-	2016	-	-
INFO-CALLTIME	-	0	-	-
REF-CALLTIME	-	0	-	-
INQU-CALLTIME	-	248	-	-
DOC-CS-CALLTIME	-	2264	-	-
TOTAL-CALLTIME	-	2264	-	-
CA-TAX	-	0	-	-
CREDIT-CARD	-	7	-	-
NY-TAX	-	0	-	-
REBUT-I-NO	-	7	-	-
UPSELL-2-NO	-	7	-	-
ANI-CAPTURE	-	8	-	-
C/S-1	-	0	-	-
C/S-2	-	1	-	-
C/S-3	-	0	-	-
C/S-4	-	0	-	-
C/S-5	-	0	-	-
DOC-INQ-1	-	0	-	-
DOC-INQ-2	-	0	-	-

```
ICSC6010 Ver. 01                          ( Source Code Hour Report )          ORDER DATE: 01/15/04
                                                                                RUN DATE: 01/16/04    PAGE:    2

CLIENT NUMBER -403200
PRODUCT ID - STIKI       PRODUCT DESCRIPTION - STIKIBOARD
SOURCE ------------------------------------------------- HOURS -------------------------------------------------
 CODE    0000 0100 0200 0300 0400 0500 0600 0700 0800 0900 1000 1100 1200 1300 1400 1500 1600 1700 1800 1900 2000 2100 2200 2300 TOTAL
DOC-INQ-3    -    -    -    -    0 U.S. -    -    -    0 CANADA -    0
DOC-INQ-4    -    -    -    -    0 U.S. -    -    -    0 CANADA -    0
DOC-INQ-5    -    -    -    -    0 U.S. -    -    -    0 CANADA -    0
DOC-INQ-6    -    -    -    -    7 U.S. -    -    -    7 CANADA -    0
TOTAL-QUANTITY -  -    -    -    5 U.S. -    -    -    5 CANADA -    0
UPSELL-NO

The following sources did not generate any calls:
BIO        COURT        LIFE-MOVIE   OXYGEN      SOAPNET

                                    END OF PRODUCT
```

194

Appendix G

Industry Data from the Electronic Retailing Association (ERA), 2005

The following information is provided courtesy of the Electronic Retailing Association (ERA). The ERA is a great resource, bringing together representatives from throughout the industry, from inventors and marketing companies to media buyers, telemarketing companies, producers, fulfillment centers, and even the QVCs and HSNs of the world. The ERA provides a forum for sharing ideas, discussing opportunities, and working to overcome obstacles for like-minded individuals from around the globe, all with the same goal—to sell products and generate revenues in an honest and ethical manner.

ERA'S FACTS AND STATISTICS ON THE DIRECT RESPONSE INDUSTRY, 2005

- Direct response was a $296 billion industry in 2004 (this included DR TV, radio, and the Internet), with a growth rate of 8 percent over the previous year.
- Of the total for 2004, $167 billion was attributed to direct response television only, which included infomercials. In 2003,

$154 billion was attributed to DR TV, which indicated a growth rate of 8 percent as well.

- The prior year, in 2003, the complete direct response was estimated as a $256 billion industry, with a growth rate of 10 percent since 2002.
- Between 2003 and 2004, the direct response industry grew by 15.6 percent.
- In 2004, 2,036 infomercials ran on cable and network television; of that, 714 were new shows in 2004.
- In 2004, 51 infomercial programs ran more than 50 times, which indicated a "successful" show; this was a 7 percent success rate.
- Over 200,000 half-hour blocks of airtime were reserved on cable and network television each month.
- That's 6 million airtime minutes of infomercials each month, or 200,000 minutes a day, just in the United States alone.
- On average, through 2005, over 400 infomercials were being produced each year, or approximately 35 to 40 per month.
- Approximately $980 million was spent on buying media in 2004. (This figure included major agencies; the number was higher when it included local buys, auto dealerships, religious and humanitarian organizations, and so on.) That number was up from $930 million reported for 2003, for a growth rate of 5 percent.
- Virtually thousands of products are being sold via direct response each day to America's consumers, especially products related to health, fitness, and beauty.
- In 2004, Internet direct response sales grossed approximately $64 billion. Advertising expenditures via the Internet totaled $1.9 billion, an 8.2 percent increase over $1.8 billion last year in 2003. (However, by total dollar amount, local newspapers and network TV still led all media at $5.9 billion and $5.8 billion, respectively.)
- In 2004, total U.S. sales revenue attributed to all direct marketing, including direct mail, reached $2.3 trillion.

Appendix H

Industry Data from the Electronic Retailing Association (ERA), 2006

ERA'S FACTS AND STATISTICS ON THE DIRECT RESPONSE INDUSTRY, 2006

All Buyers

- The proportion of all adults buying through electronic channels was consistent over the last year, at 46 percent. Thirty-three percent of all adults purchased something online, 14 percent through a TV infomercial, 10 percent through home shopping, and 6 percent through radio.
- There was relatively little change in the demographic measures among all buyers. The average age was 47.1, which was an increase over 2005. Half claimed to be college graduates, and the median income was just under $57,000.
- The median amount spent on the most recent purchase stayed at $50, although due to a few very large purchases, the average climbed from $199 to $295. The median purchase price was $50 for all segments except radio, where it was $40.

- Buyers were divided over how they typically tuned into a TV program. Twenty-three percent channel surfed, 30 percent used an on-screen guide, 34 percent knew what they wanted to watch and tuned in directly, and 10 percent used a printed guide. This didn't vary tremendously by buyer segment, nor did it change from last year.
- Half of all buyers said they had watched at least one TV infomercial for at least a minute or two in the past three months, which was a drop from 59 percent last year. However, the average number of infomercials watched rose from 4.35 to 5.72 among all buyers. TV infomercial and radio buyers were the most likely to have watched an infomercial.
- Twenty percent of online purchases were impulse buys, up from 12 percent last year. Most broadcast purchases were impulse buys (66 percent for TV infomercial, 64 percent for radio, and 70 percent for home shopping).
- Fifty-six percent of all buyers said an up-sell attempt was made, including 6 percent who bought what was being offered. Overall numbers were consistent from last year, but there were changes for up-sell recall within segments: Radio went up (47 to 60 percent), while home shopping went down (54 to 41 percent).
- Fifty-two percent of all buyers would definitely consider using that same method to purchase a product in the future, while another 23 percent would probably consider this. Very few people would probably not (8 percent) or definitely not (3 percent) consider future purchases. These numbers are consistent with last year.
- In the past 12 months, 16 percent of all buyers who used the Internet said they had seen a product on a TV infomercial and then bought it online. Eight percent had seen a product on a home shopping program and bought it online, and 8 percent had done this with a radio infomercial. There was somewhat less multichannel use from broadcast to Internet this year than there was last year.

- Twenty-four percent rated their trust of offers made on 24-hour home shopping channels at a 4 or a 5 on a scale of 1 (trust not at all) to 5 (trust very much). Trust in TV commercials was the same (24 percent), while radio (19 percent), Web sites (16 percent), and TV infomercials (14 percent) were trusted even less. Trust in Web sites and TV infomercials fell from last year.

Home Shopping Buyers

- The average age was 54.4, 68 percent were female, 57 percent were married, 38 percent were college graduates, and median income was $50,455.
- Forty percent would definitely consider purchasing through home shopping again, and 26 percent would probably consider this. This was a slight drop from last year, and it was definitely down from 2004.
- Sixty-four percent of home shopping buyers said they had seen the product they bought promoted multiple times on air before buying it. In addition, 21 percent had seen the product promoted in another medium (mostly in a store, a magazine ad, or a newspaper ad). This was all consistent with last year.
- Fifty-four percent of home shopping buyers had bought from the same company in addition to this most recent purchase, which was about the same as last year.
- Just 16 percent could not recall the name of the home shopping program or channel they used most recently; the most common were QVC (60 percent) and HSN (14 percent). However, 42 percent could not recall the channel number of that channel.

TV Infomercial Buyers

- The average age was 52.0, 60 percent were female, 60 percent were married, 37 percent were college graduates, and median income was $52,059.
- Twenty-one percent would definitely consider purchasing through a TV infomercial again, and 26 percent would probably consider this. This was somewhat of a drop from last year.
- Eighty-six percent of TV infomercial buyers said they had seen the product they bought promoted multiple times on air before buying it. In addition, 32 percent had seen the product promoted in another medium (usually in a store, in magazines, and/or through newspaper ads). This was all consistent with last year.
- Fifteen percent of TV infomercial buyers had bought from the same company in addition to this most recent purchase, which was up about the same as last year.
- For their most recent purchase, 45 percent of TV infomercial buyers used a short-form infomercial, and 48 percent used a long-form infomercial.

Index

About the Author

Michael Planit has more than 20 years of strategic business and marketing experience with a broad-based exposure in product/brand licensing.

With a strong track record of success, Michael's products have achieved in excess of $125 million in wholesale sales in the past few years alone.

Largely through his position as president of Product Strategies, Inc., he has developed and consulted on numerous consumer products in categories including household, hardware, skincare, and novelty products. He has worked directly on the creation, acquisition, and/or marketing of many successful products within the Infomercial arena.

These products include the Boogie Bass novelty singing fish (2000 "No. 1 Short-form Product"), DermaFresh skincare products, the Trikke (*Time for Kids* magazine's 2002 "Best Invention"), the Smart Tape digital tape measure (2003 "Best Product" award, Electronic Retailing Association), the EdgeMaster, the GripWrench, the Over Easy Flip Pan, and many more.

Michael has recently been added to the adjunct faculty at New York University (NYU) to teach a core curriculum course, *Mastering New Product and Service Development,* for their Marketing Certificate Program. In addition, he was recently appointed to chair the New Product Hot Spot Task Force for the Electronic Retailing Association (ERA).

Additionally, Michael founded Creative Zone, a toy and novelty manufacturer of various children's products through all major retail channels, founded on a licensed product concept that he developed featuring licenses from Warner Bros., Marvel, Nickelodeon, and the NBA. Prior to Creative Zone, he spearheaded the turnaround of what became the nation's second largest contract sweater manufacturer.

He resides in New York City with his wife and three children, and is very involved with the community and various children's charity organizations.

To contact Product Strategies:

for individuals: inventors@productstrategies.com

for companies: products@productstrategies.com